The Awful Truth

Diana Hamilton

GOLIAS BOOKS

The Awful Truth

An excerpt of "Write In Your Sleep" appeared in *Convolution*, and an excerpt of "Fear and Trembling" in *Rabbit*. Parts of this manuscript were written as a writer-in-residence at the Blackacre Nature Conservancy for the Baltic Writer's Residency and as a resident at BHQFU.

Printed in Michigan by McNaughton & Gunn
First printing, 2017

ISBN-13: 978-0-9994-3131-3

The text is set in Janson, a typeface originally designed by Miklós Tótfalusi Kis after the Dutch Baroque style.

The cover is set in GT Sectra and Perpetua.

The Golias Books device is taken from an illustration by François Desprez, spuriously attributed to Rabelais, in *Les Songes drolatiques de Pantagruel* (1565).

Designed and published by Golias Books

www.goliasbooks.com

N. Y.   N. C.

If the artist (in whatever medium) is searching for the self, then it can be said that in all probability there is already some failure for that artist in the field of general creative living.

—D.W. Winnicott, Playing and Reality

Our problem is that we think too much. All day, all night. At night, we call it dreaming. Everyone dreams. We can't stop the dreams any more than the thoughts. Since we can't stop them, we must be more aware of them. To be conscious of these thoughts and conscious of these dreams: 'The sea can be violent or still . . . It follows no pattern' . . . 'My family is very ordinary.' Heaven, Hell, virtue, sin are nothing but suppositions.

—Apichatpong Weerasethakul, Cemetery of Splendour

That's it. That's as far as I've gotten. I've left alot out of this, including alot of dreams but the dreams often provide me with the words I need to work from. I havent finished anything but I have the idea that if I now take a space & inundate that space with words, all the words that have come out of this, set it up so that the words can be looked at, read & listened, all at once, for days, hours, the observers, or the audience, would be in a corner, pushed into a corner, into being me, or just into me. Anyway its a good question.

—Bernadette Mayer, Studying Hunger

This book is dedicated to my blankets:
- *Mimi*
- *The plaid comforter I slept atop to avoid making the bed*
- *My brother's cat blanket, which I tried to steal*
- *The throw with the Xmas landscape I bought because its texture was like Ryan's cat blanket*
- *The quilt from my parents' bed, which I sadly threw out when Easy-the-cat shat on it*
- *The quilt from Anthropologie's "Semiologie by A.P.C." line, lol*
- *The one my mom crocheted for me in high school*
- *The one I crocheted for an ex, who threw it away when he felt called to abandon all possessions*

Write in Your Sleep

Some say we shouldn't describe our dreams.

I say: fuck that.

But saying "fuck that" won't persuade everyone.

Instead, I'll prove it with "research"

about dreams & wishes. Specifically, two:
the wish to write, the wish to feel better.

Here's an annotated bibliography
on how, when we dream, we write:

—if lazily, in fear or love, without credentials.
In *Venus in Furs*, "the story is set in motion by a dream

that occurs during an interrupted reading."[1] (So's this.)
An unnamed man tells Severin his dream
of "speaking to Venus about love while she wears furs"[2]
who, among her many cruelties, tells *him* that he, and his people,

"do not know what love is about." Severin listens
under a painting of the same woman—"That is how I saw her
in my dreams," the narrator exclaims; "But I was dreaming
with my eyes open," says Severin[3]—

---

[1] Gilles Deleuze, *Masochosim: Coldness and Cruelty*, trans. Jean McNeil (Boston: MIT Press, 1971), 22.

[2] Wikipedia contributors, "Venus in Furs," *Wikipedia* https://en.wikipedia.org/w/index.php?title=Venus_in_Furs&oldid=780633396

[3] Leopold Sacher von Masoch, *Venus in Furs*, in Deleuze's *Masochism*, 148.

and recommends he read a book about it. (Good advice.)
Bob Glück, in *About Ed*, says "I slept
so lightly I complained in my dreams
about still being awake."[4] He dreams of his lover

helping him paint the loft, buy a bathtub, Denny
with an unruly dog, and as he writes the dream
down, he understands it "means that Ed was giving [him] a hand
with this book." Freud says he's nervous

he's not a poet given how much
of himself he's about to tell.[5]
Same. Writers should go to sleep
when they need help:

> Hamilton, Diana. "Onion Poet's Dream, on the eve of her birth-
> day." Email message to therapist. December 7, 2013.

> Hamilton dreams that she is at a party of older poets. They are
> collaborating on an impressive dish she does not want because
> she has chronic IBS.

> To contribute, she makes her "specialty," which is a big loaf of
> hearty bread, cut into slices with an onion spread. She demon-
> strates how to make it: it's just an onion, cut in a secret way
> that, when unlocked, reveals units of paste instead of slices—as
> if you roasted a head of garlic and cut it in half. All of the older
> poets are impressed, and though they are from many different
> countries, they all say it reminds them of a food they had in their
> childhood and that they would rather have it than the fancy
> meal that is coming.

---

[4] Robert Glück, reading at the Poetry Project at St. Mark's Church in the Bowery, December 7, 2016.

[5] Sigmund Freud, *The Interpretation of Dreams*, trans. James Strachey (New York: Basic Books, 2010), xxiv.

In the dream, Hamilton forgets that, in real life, she stopped eating onions once she developed the IBS; i.e., her dip is a terrible solution.

Yet in her sleep, she writes a story that
1. minimizes the work women put into preparing food,
2. earns her the attention of her elders, and
3. rejects luxury in favor of sustenance.

Describing a dream is like reading the first draft
of a poem aloud to a friend who didn't offer to listen:

It's rude. But it's a fine way to force someone
to help you get over writer's block.

Dreams appear among Bernadette Mayer's
"experiments." She says to

> Write down your dreams as the first thing you do every morning for 30 days. Apply translation and aleatoric processes to this material. Double the length of each dream. Weave them together into one poem, adding or changing or reordering material. Negate or reverse all statements ("I went down the hill" to "I went up the hill," "I didn't" to "I did"). Borrow a friend's dreams and apply these techniques to them.[6]

I did this on accident: I wrote dream notes on a whiteboard to see what "came together," and what came together was love:

> A lover was a book by me, I had written
> him, but he was still man-sized and book-sized. He wanted me
> to inscribe him to him, an act I've always hated,
> and hate requesting. For this reason

[6] Bernadette Mayer, "Bernadette Mayer's Writing Experiments," accessed May 27, 2016, http://www.writing.upenn.edu/library/Mayer-Bernadette_Experiments.html

I'll only do it when it feels urgent: I saw
Bernadette Mayer in Oakland recently, and I couldn't
help but ask her to sign my copy of *Ethics of Sleep*
because I love her more than all poets
who have ever existed and that was the book I had
just bought. I told her I loved her. She laughed
and asked for a sip of my beer. I gave her one
from my bag. One thing you might not know is that
Bernadette Mayer is the most beautiful human. She asked me:
"So you like my work. Should I keep writing?"

I hesitated. I said, "Of course, selfishly, I want
to say yes. But you should do whatever the fuck
you want." She threw her head back
and laughed again as she opened the beer. "You know
I can't sign my name since my stroke?"
She wrote "BM" in block letters. I said, "yes."

When people ask me to sign a book I feel
like they are asking me to revise it, to come up
with a line that was left out by mistake, and that line
is the one where I would have made it clear
that I love them, in advance. In my dream,
the book/lover that I had written specifically
asked me to inscribe him, "I love you, _____,"
where that blank is his name, you get it.
I wrote "Dream where D is book I wrote, ILY"
on the whiteboard, lived another day, went back
to sleep, dreamt of another lover, who, in the dream,
had my body. Specifically, I saw her belly fat
hang in the same way mine hangs: stretch marks
having loosened the skin such that, in any position
other than lying flat on my/her back, it sags
low, and, since neither me nor
this dream lover is so insecure that we would

avoid the kinds of sex where your belly hangs
for the sake of vanity, I watched her belly swing,
I thought, "I didn't know she had the same body
as me, that's surprising, from here, on her,
it's hot, I want her even more than I would
if her belly were tight." This is a lie: in real life,
she is too beautiful and no skin hangs, and because
I like her, I like these things about her,
too, I'm glad she doesn't have my body, but
there I was: one lover was my body, the other my book,
I just need to sleep with someone new
who can be my mind, I guess; from other's dreams, I get
the sense it could be useful to have one
who is my mom or my dad, too.

Remember the opening to *Midwinter Day*:

Stately you came to town in my opening dream
Lately you've been showing up alot
                                        I saw clearly
You were staying in the mirror with me
You walk in, the hills are green, I keep you warm
Placed in this cold country in a town of mountains
Replaced from that balmier city of yours near the sea
Now it's your turn to fall down from the love of my look
You stayed in the hotel called your daughter's arms
No wonder the mother's so forbidding, so hard to embrace
I only wait in the lobby, in the bar
                                        I write
People say, "What is it?"
I ask if I must tell all the rest
For never, since I was born
and for no man or woman I've ever met,
I'll swear to that,
Have there been such dreams as I had today,

The 22nd day of December,
Which, as I can now remember,
I'll tell you all about, if I can

                    Can I say what I saw

In sleep in dreams[7]

You want to write, "Yes, of course, Bernadette,"
in the margin but she's playing you: she doesn't
need your permission to write this book, just as
she didn't need mine to write whatever she will
or won't in the coming years, but
this is her dream: "People all around me / Wondering
what it is I write"—she's dreaming and writing
of a needy reader, a lover who shows up alot.
It's the dream itself that permits you
to write it. Dreams are more confident than
poets, they don't wait to win prizes
from the Poetry Society of America:

> Hamilton, Diana. "Dream in which the Poetry Society of
> America mistakenly gives me a prize." Email to self. April
> 27, 2016.

> Hamilton is sitting in the basement of an event space where
> people approach her to let her know she's been awarded a large
> prize by the Poetry Society of America.

> She explains that there's no way it's her, she didn't even apply,
> and anyway, she doesn't write the kind of poems that win those
> prizes. They point to her name on the envelope and show her
> that it says "Diana Hamilton," but it has a different person's
> address and phone number. She explains that there are a lot of
> people named Diana Hamilton. But she can't convince them it's
> not her, and they show her their poorly formatted spreadsheet,
> which says "Diana Hamilton—*OK, OK*," the title is misspelled

---

[7] Bernadette Mayer, *Midwinter Day* (New York: New Directions, 1999), 1-2.

and she knows it's not for her. She wants to be left alone. She explains that whoever filled out their spreadsheet probably researched the title of the writers' books *after* making the spreadsheet, so it doesn't mean anything. They try to give her the envelope announcing the prize anyway, because they've only been tasked with making the deliveries.

And, they explain, they've been looking for her "forever."

That's when Hamilton's ex shows up and gives her a second envelope, this one full of all of the letters and scraps of paper she ever wrote to him, including printed emails, as if he's trying to get more money for the linear feet of his archive, and because he "doesn't need them anymore." She can't take this, so she goes to the bathroom to hide from the need to cry, but someone is following her, she knows they are going to attack her, she tries to hide by crouching over a toilet seat. Once hidden, she realizes that whoever is following her only has to open each stall in turn to find her, so she gives up, she falls on the floor and cries anyway, this time from fear and sadness. By the time they find her, they are no longer a villain, they are the ex, they are a villain, they get in a car together and she has to run errands but again she can't take it, gets out of the car with her envelopes and runs, but the car catches up to her, not on purpose, just because walking is slow, and she is humiliated but gets back in.

It seems generous of the dream to have selected me
for the prize, but the dream is actually too busy being proud
of its own ability to give prizes to worry about me or my book[8]
about crying, often in the bathroom stall. Diana,
your feelings will find you wherever you run and wherever you pee,
leave your book behind, you have processing to do, run faster.

I am not the first poet to have been awarded a large prize by falling
asleep.

---

[8] Diana Hamilton, *Okay, Okay* (Queens, NY: Truck Books, 2012).

It also happened to Ted Berrigan,
a fact I forgot, but surely remembered
on some level when the Poetry Society came calling:

> I've been dreaming. The telephone kept ringing & ringing
> Clear & direct, purposeful yet pleasant, still taking pleasure
> in bringing the good news, a young man in horn-rims' voice
> > is speaking
> while I listen. Mr. Berrigan, he says, & without waiting for an
> > answer goes on,
> I'm happy to be able to inform you that your request for a
> > Guggenheim Foundation Grant
> Has been favorably received by the committee, & approved.
> > When would you like to leave?[9]

Of course, this is an entirely different dream: Berrigan is a man
for whom the receipt of a large prize comes naturally,
even if a kind of self-deprecation marks the whole description.
Though too lazy to have outlined a project—the glasses-wearing
voice says

> > . . . You indicated, wisely, I think, that we knew
> > more about what kind of project we would approve than you did
> > so we should
> > make one up for you, since all you wanted was money . . .

—he doesn't try to say no. He prepares to leave. I am worried
now that to write about dreams is to be a New York School Poet.
A Larry comes to Frank O'Hara in one of "Two Dreams
of Waking" and says "I'm / glad you're developing breasts,"
and the friend sitting beside me, Joey Yearous-Algozin, the one
who told me to read "Something Amazing Just Happened" when
I asked

[9] Ted Berrigan, "Something Amazing Just Happened," *Selected Poems* (New York:
Penguin Books, 1994), 59.

him to tell me about a poem about a dream, can tell me it's Larry
Rivers. I could only avoid being a NYSP in this section by telling you
Joey's last name is Yearous-Algozin. Yearous-Algozin
tells me that, if I were his student, and I asked him
"What is the New York School of Poetry like?" he would
respond "how did you hear about that?" and then he would say

> It's both really obsessed with art and formalism
> as it's simultaneously obsessed with the non-profound confession.
> It's interested in the surfaces of relationships as people move
>   between them.[10]

Then he says something about how the city does this
because there are all these friends you don't know well
even though you see them every Friday at a reading,
or something—he says he doesn't want to be closer
to these poets. If I were his student
I would be very confused right now.

> I would tell them, just read O'Hara and selected Barbara Guest,
> and Ashbery doesn't apply. That's not fair to Schuyler,

he says.

> The main thing I would say is, 'why am I sitting on your couch,
>   student?'

I am not having a dream in which I am Joey's confused student
and we are having an affair.

*

---

[10] Joey Yearous-Algozin (poet) in discussion with author, November 1, 2016.

The "Poetry and Dream" exhibit at the Tate
Modern suggests that dreams, like poetry,
are too generic: both can include the entirety
of a century's art, fiction, found objects, etc.: for Joan Miró's
1927 *Painting*,[11] the wall text describes how
"Delicate linear forms float on the open blue
that Miró associated with dreams." Dreams are mere colors
and shapes, here; they don't tell stories. Someone important
to me objects that "float" is a story, but this is giving verbs
a lot of credit, in my opinion; I'll grant that it's in between;
rather, dreams, for Miró, can aspire to become sentences
in addition to becoming paintings. Miró thought,
according to this description, that dreams were simple:

> From this he developed his own personal sign language, which
> simplified familiar things such as stars, birds, and parts of the
> body. He later revealed, for example, that the white shape in this
> painting signified a horse.[12]

How useful of dreams to make a horse-shape mean
horse, the word "bird" wasn't functioning
until it became bird-shaped in open blue,
that's for sure, *ugh*, art is dull, "Poetry and Dream" prioritized
    surrealists,
for whom dreams were too dreamy. I don't mean writing melting
clocks, coded abstract shapes, or metaphor sans reference,
I just mean writing stories. Another poet dreamt:

---

[11] Joan Miró, Painting, 1927, water-soluble background and motifs in oil, on canvas,
38 ¼ in. x 51 ¼ in., Tate Modern, London.

[12] "Catalogue entry," accessed May 27, 2016, http://www.tate.org.uk/art/artworks/
miro-painting-t01318/text-catalogue-entry

Anonymous poet. "Family Prophecy Dream." Personal journal.
June 1999.

The poet/dreamer's Uncle Steve says: "Remember, there is a
prophecy that the first grandchild would abandon the God of
his family."

I don't know whether this poet is the first grandchild, but he
certainly becomes it in his dream—or he becomes the abandoned
God or family, becomes the white horse-shape or whatever
animal-shape gave the prophecy—and I'll imagine that this
dream came with a sense of relief. *It has been written*, a prophecy
promises, there's no need to do anything other than live this one
out, bb, it's in the stars. "Remember," the dream says—I love
it when dreams remind you that they are revising, rather than
writing.

The poet Shiv Kotecha is sitting across from me
right now, he says one of the dreams
he had last night was that
he had all of these beautiful clothes.
When he got home this morning
he went to put them on and
he was disappointed.[13] In another dream
he was taking a cat video of Monster, our cat,
but there was fire coming out of his mouth,
the cat had a giant purple halo.
"I took this video and I couldn't find it
in the morning, it sucked," he says.
He can see that I'm still typing while he talks
so he apologizes for interrupting me but
I ask him to keep going, "I'm writing
my annotated bibliography of dreams,"
I tell him. He tells me, "It's a law of physics that
that which is being observed will change."

[13] Shiv Kotecha (poet) in discussion with author, April 20, 2016.

"I hope you're texting this to a boy, *baby*," he adds
in a funny voice. I keep typing, and it's hard to
type awake because you know what you're typing
won't be usable, whereas in sleep, you don't know
that the thing you're writing doesn't exist
until you wake up:

"I muar ve w hifh"

ahic sowan'r knoq I'm qeokinf on rhw NNORWSrw sviflio-
vfepH OD SEWma nS ARera ro rwll mw VOUR HIA SEWma

I xn'R AWW RHW AXEWWN AO I SON'R KNOQ QHr I'm
rypinf nS Rhr xhNFWA RHW DWWLINFA vour rhw qoesa
rhR PPWe, ir'a moew VOUR RHW PLWauew od rypinf irawld

id youe dinfwea kwwp mocinf you xn'R Ay rhR YOU'EW NOR
FWRRINF nyrhinf sonw

vur ir'a heS RO MinriN RHIA IEL DOE CWEY LONF
VWXuaw you vwxomw Qew rhR YOU ewn'r qeirinf nYRHINF
YOU QILL UAW

IN sewm YOU SOSN'R EWliW rhw rhinf rhw qeorw sowan'r
wcwn wziar unril you qkW UP[14]

That's what I actually wrote while Shiv talked,
because my fingers moved to the left on the keyboard
without my noticing,

because waking life doesn't work
any better than sleep, it's just more boring.

*

---

[14] Diana Hamilton, email message to author, April 20, 2016.

I don't mean "dream" as in "aspiration" as in "I dream of growing up
    to be a writer."

And yet.

In addition to this more figurative dream, which I had too, I admit,
I also literally dreamt of books I had written. You've had this
dream: you have written a book, too, it's a terrific book
and you are its terrific writer, perhaps you, like 12-year-old me,
wrote a novel in your sleep, one where the letters
sometimes became pictures, so they meant what the words
took the shape of rather than what the words said, for example,
or you dreamt that you had written a book someone else
already wrote, perhaps a scary book about trees
and mystery, you woke up, you tried to write it down.

Yes, yes, yes, I know, we can't remember
details when we wake, writing is not special,
you want to say, this is not interesting Dr. Hamilton.

But waking up from having written a book is *worse*.

Listen, it's worse even than waking up
from having dreamt of sex you can't remember: with the latter
you still have the impression you had sex on waking—you might long
to recall the details, you might open your phone to look at a photo
from two summers ago that was secretly a picture of a person's eyes
to whom you were desperately attracted, yes, it's painful
that you can't remember the kisses you know you just had and
that you'll never get to have awake, but this is not as painful as the book
you dreamt you wrote but can't recall, because—

their non-existence is to a different degree.
You wake up to learn that you didn't write the book *at all*, not even a
    dream book,
that your dream misunderstood what it meant to "write a book," it didn't
last long enough to experience the full awful years of coming up with
    a bad idea,
fleshing it out, revising it, writing through the night, traveling to
    another city
in hopes that you'll remember how to write if you leave town,
    showing it to a friend,
having the friend pretend to like it unsuccessfully, having something
    happen to you
that leads you to go for more walks which leads you
to have more ideas which leads you to return to the initial idea,
computer shutting down mid-draft or saving so many alternate
    versions you can't
resolve them into one text, falling asleep getting off and dreaming
    of kisses
you'll never have that you hope to write into the book, writing them in,
rereading those kisses in the drafts for two years, removing
    the kisses
when you're still trying to finish the goddamn book at a point where
    you're over
the kisses or at least the would-be kisser, sending it to a prize, etc.
Dreams are lazy. This is why they are great writers, this is why they
    never write
books in the dreams themselves; they only offer the dream content
    "wrote a book"
with few actual pages, which can be turned into real pages only by
    disrespect
for the dream and its non-existent book and its failure to know
    what books are.

Dreams do more than write, though. They also cheat:

Oerman, Ashley. "What it Really Means if You're Dreaming About an Ex." *Women's Health*, 5/28/2014. Accessed May 27, 2016. http://www.womenshealthmag.com/sex-and-love/dreams-about-your-ex

Proceeding from the discovery that "Americans are more likely to dream about an ex than their current partner," Oerman tries to determine, for the sake of the readership of *Women's Health*, whether it's "cheating" to dream of an ex (the article does not specify sex dreams, so it suggests some readers might worry simply thinking about another man constitutes infidelity). She consults a PhD or two to determine that it is "very normal."

This article fails to address *how* to produce dreams about exes, though. It does not refer to one of the most important resources on this subject: D.H.'s "Dream Where Ex-boyfriend Slowly Drowns at the Bottom of the Shower While I Hold Him Down With My Foot and Eat Chocolate Pudding, Letting the Pudding Drip All Over Both of Our Bodies, Smiling."

Instead, it focuses on the quality of a woman's current partnership, and recommends "assessing how happy you are with your partner in all aspects of your relationship—you know, while you're awake."

In this, Oerman seems to suggest that dreaming is *not* writing; it's a way to ensure you stay with a man you won't even have interesting dreams about until you dump him.

I want to have this unfaithful, permissible sex with you.

I want to dream-write in reverse:
to write out the dream before bed
and then have it, pleasantly.

Quit smoking, smoke in your dreams,
quit seeing her, see her in your dreams, and so on:

> Hamilton, Diana. "Dream Where Ex-boyfriend Slowly Drowns
> at the Bottom of the Shower While I Hold Him Down With
> My Foot and Eat Chocolate Pudding, Letting the Pudding
> Drip All Over Both of Our Bodies, Smiling." August 2010.

This dream had a dramatic effect on Hamilton's ability to "move
on," as they say, in that her waking smile matched the showering
one, and it listed all the ways single life is like dropping chocolate
pudding without care on the corpses of your former loves.

Her dream made solid writerly decisions. Like Barthes, the dream
understands that what may seem at first like "a kind of narrative
luxury, lavish to the point of offering many futile 'details' and
thereby increasing the cost of narrative information,"[15] actually
produces the *reality effect*. Barthes's example is Flaubert's placing
of a barometer over a piano, in a descriptive sentence where
everything else can be accounted for by the structure, but where
the barometer seems excessive. What's great about dreams, in fact,
is that it's much harder to tell which signifiers are "meaningful"
(the pudding resembles shit, and you dream only about shit; it's
a reference to some sort of excrement of feelings, or to comfort
with defecation and consumption) and which simply fill in
some blank space that requires something "real"—producing a
difference between "eating unspecified food in the shower" or
"eating chicken in the shower" or "eating hot lentil soup in the
shower," etc.

Dreams are great at producing these little references to the fact
that there's something to be referenced. Freud leaves the "navel"

---

[15] Roland Barthes, "The Reality Effect," in *The Novel: An Anthology of Criticism and
Theory 1900:2000*, ed. by Dorothy Hale (New York: John Wiley & Sons, 2009), 230.

[16] Freud, *Interpretation*, 528.

of the dream obscure because "it adds nothing to our knowledge of the content of the dream. The dream's navel is the spot where it reaches down in the unknown."[16]

The dream does not have to google "dream's navel" to remember this. It writes without needing academic support. But if it had, it would be reminded that this quote is very frustrating, because, as the internet points out, Freud also says of the Wolf Man's dream that "it is always a strict law of dream interpretation that an explanation must be found for every detail."[17] Regardless of which Freud you believe, which Barthes, which Hamilton, which food, the beauty of the dream is that it doesn't need to furnish that explanation; it doesn't experience writer's block. The dream is so comforted by having chosen one *you* to address that it doesn't need to worry over interpretation—it's an act of love from the dream to Hamilton.

Consider being awake: A man you love leaves you.

You could add "suddenly," "terribly," "out of the blue,"
"with groceries in my arms as I came home to make him dinner,"
"for a mother who [identifying details removed],"
but the more specific the identifying details—the "effects of reality"—
the greater the sense this has been "difficult."

You add details: you want the difficulty understood.

You remove them: you want ease.

You look for a way to end the sentence
there: "A man you loved leaves you."

---

[17] Sigmund Freud, *An Infantile Neurosis and Other Works (1917–1919)*, trans. James Strachey (New York: Vintage Classics, 2001), 17.

Asleep, you would never remember you had started the sentence and so would be spared ending it:

> Hamilton, Diana. "Fragment of Dream with Mistaken Boyfriend." Note to self. April 10, 2016.

> The archive only maintains a small fragment of this dream, which opens onto Hamilton at her computer, laughing happily, high, and typing up the events of the day in an email to her boyfriend (IRL ex). Shiv enters the room and expresses surprise she's writing to him: "I thought you were never going to talk to him again?"

> "Oh shit!" she says, laughing, and closes the computer, tossing it onto the chaise. She thanks him for reminding her.

> Here, we hit upon the limits of these materials, which we can only access through the dreamer's transcription. The dream itself cannot possibly have written so positively, so we take this not as evidence of the dream's actual ability to process loss, but as evidence of the way our mediation of dreams on waking has curative functions similar to diaries; in both, we pretend to document wishes, feelings, longings, or regrets, but we instead write them into existence.

Awake, you still have hope.

You recognize your own edit,
"love" to "loved" (we also write while awake).

But you don't get the pleasure of being relaxed.

*

I had another poetry dream:

I was in bed with a poet
where I try not to be these days,
and we were just sleeping as friends
until he started to try to get me off.
I was shocked that this particular poet
was good at it, I came before I could rethink
whether it was a good idea to be in this bed,
in this poet's hands. As I came, a large egg sac,
slimy and malleable like the ball of burrata
I had for lunch the day the before, came out of me.
At first, I thought it was my own normal personal
residue, which I tried to explain, but as I held it
in my hands, I realized there was something inside, and
I threw it on the floor, where it split to reveal
a head of lettuce wrapped in paper towels
that looked as though it was from the farmer's market.
I woke up, not to my real bed, but to the poet's,
a dream within a dream, I admitted, "I just had a weird
sex dream about you," and he said, "me too" and
he finished telling the story for me, how we picked
the head of lettuce off the floor and washed it,
discussed the salad we would have. I woke up
again, this time for real, and texted the dream to Sophia,
who misunderstood, thought that I had actually slept over
at the poet's, I had to correct her, only then did I see
that I had given birth to a Cabbage Patch Kid, impregnated
by the hand of a writer whose work is all about gross monogamy
and the desire for children. I woke up again, this time
more figuratively, to think about all this dream sex and dream
dancing with poets, what kind of lettuce head I think it will lead to.

What am I afraid of, here? I am afraid

that if I read a book about monogamy I will write a book
about monogamy, or I will wake up to find myself heterosexual,
or I will value heterosexuality as a way to produce children, which
I will Create by letting a Monogamous Man make a promise
as to the likelihood of our being happy with our Cabbage Patch
Kid, i.e., the book of poetry we will co-write
about the meaningfulness of being parents, or by letting
a non-monogamous person make a promise as to the likelihood
of our being happy with our lettuce head, i.e., perpetual cunnilingus
as a stand-in for love that can stand the test of reading
books about other loves, which creates the temptation to fall
in love anew rather than to continue loving
by going down on the extant already-loved person beside you,
or I will wake up to find myself, as I often do
in dreams, with a real human child whose other parent I have
abandoned so as not to trap them into life with me
and the child, who is crying, as am I, on the other side
of the apartment, where I attempt to write or otherwise
do the things my dream imagines will be difficult or less
likely in this lettuce head baby future,
where a child with whom we might even dance
might one day dream of writing themself.

I fear, I mean, that I will become a mom, mine, I am
becoming her by becoming one, that's one step closer,
without the dream lettuce I'd be safer.

I fear that my "personal residue" is disgusting.

I fear that, if I read a book, I will write the book,
or I will wake up to find myself desirous of writing
a book other than the ones I'm capable of writing,
that if I eat the burrata, I will not only secrete the burrata
in my dreams but also in poems, "You are what you eat"

standing in for the question of whether, if what I've eaten
is all the books I read in grad school, where a class on "being"
includes no writing by people who aren't white men, suggesting
no one else "exists," where your own ideas are taken seriously
only when voiced again by the man who tried to assault "you,"
as a writer who shits out the burrata without rendering it
sufficiently unrecognizable because I failed to shit it out
through my ass but instead through dream-orgasm, I will come
to resemble all this intake, I will only be able to write the shit
I agreed to read. Reading is writing
just as much as dreaming is, be careful, don't be careful,
that is, be careful by not being too careful, there's no way
you'll choose the right things to eat or read or kiss, so
it's safest to eat and read and kiss as much as possible
to increase the likelihood you'll encounter the most
nutrient-rich book or kiss or lettuce. They used to tell you not to
eat some lettuces because they had "nothing" in them
but it's not a bad idea to encounter nothing from time to time.

*

Speaking of moms,
they write their children's dreams:

SOMEONE'S DREAMS ABOUT THEIR MOM
---. "Mom is an alcoholic watching me have a lesbian orgy at
   JCPenney."
---. "Mom reenrolled me in a high school math class that's too
   easy."
---. "Mom and dad fight off an army of skeletons trying to break
   into my bedroom."

If you believe me that our mom dreams are given
to us by our mothers, you believe that other dreams might be, too,
in the sense that dreams are a kind of inheritance.

Hamilton, Diana. Dream in Scotland.

Hamilton is hanging out with a friend she's visiting
(IRL and in the dream)
and somehow a story he's telling requires him to simulate

rape. He's on the floor with another man—
a man she finds disgusting, but the important thing is
that the friend puts himself in the position of the victim,

talks the guy through the motions of holding him down, face to
   the ground, etc.
The whole thing is very friendly, and everyone stays dressed, but
   at the same time it
gives Hamilton a sense of what they would both be like undressed.

In another image, she is in the position
of the attacker. She holds him; it's almost like spooning,
but he's also instructing her on the position she should take
for rape, it's violent.

Sometimes it feels sweet, though, sometimes
comical, sometimes traumatic, like
she's really trying to hurt him. They switch roles.
Things change, for the worse.
He is or they are both too turned on, etc.
—things are messy, it's unclear

if the violence is playacting anymore, or endable, there's
a general sense of frenzy and pawing, etc., things go
from there. The rest of the dream is confusing—
this "accident" alternates between being assault
and a motivation for them to confess their desire.

But periodically, in the dream, they try again.
Each time they find themselves by accident in someone else's
hotel room, and women keep walking in on them.

Hamilton woke up thinking, "He raped me."

She couldn't get back to sleep; she was alert. She heard her door
shake and for a moment thought it was the same
friend coming to be with her,
as if he had dreamt the same thing

[When he woke up that morning, he told her about a dream he
had during the night about mudwrestling with beautiful women
on a pirate ship.

She had been sleeping on her back, which she never does,
and which they had agreed (awake) was difficult
because it does not involve any motherly smothering].

*

Moms write our dreams because they miss us:
they want to show up to tell us something
we've done wrong.

Something she's seen.

News she has to deliver.

> Anonymous. "My mom finally figured out that I've been smoking
> weed since age 14." Dream. Date unknown.

... and she got so sad when I told her it's because she decided not
to medicate me for ADD, OCD, and anxiety as a child. She said
she blamed herself for my delinquency and she thought she was
a failure as a parent. I told her it was chill and she said 'nothing is
chill' and then I woke up.

Dads don't write dreams, but they do appear in them:

> Hamilton, Diana. "Dream where Connor and I are stoned and
> shopping with our dads," email to self, May 25, 2016.

Hamilton is shopping at Beacon's Closet with her dad, who is
visiting town, and trying to hide from him the fact that she is very
high. She is touching the clothes and trying to keep her smile
normal. She runs into Connor, who is also shopping for clothes
with her dad, and they look at each other, at first to recognize the
absurdity of the fact that they both decided to take their fathers
shopping, then to introduce each other to the dads—but as they
meet each other's eyes, they immediately see that the other is too
stoned, and they fall onto the floor and laugh with joy.

---. "Dream where Connor and I slow-dance in a ballroom."
   Recurring.

Connor appears as a character in Hamilton's dreams for many
months after her stoner-comedy introduction. She takes on a role
no one yet has: she never appears, in this initial dream-period,
as a stressful element, and in fact, she has a palliative function.
Often, when a dream becomes stressful, she appears and begins
to dance with Hamilton, in the sort of dream that a dreamer
experiences at the same pace as the experience itself; she wakes
up to the sensation that she has actually been ballroom dancing
through the night. Unlike her other dreams, where meaning is
emphasized by repetition or where the dream fails to keep to one
narrative, these dancing scenes are durational, like art movies
or like short flashbacks from sweeter movies where a snippet of
a childhood memory implies that the remembering itself lasts
much longer and represents a lost happiness.

Rather, Connor is Psalm 30:11 to her dreams: "You have turned
my mourning into dancing; you took off my sackcloth and
clothed me with a garment of joy."

There is very little mention of dancing in Freud's *Interpretation
of Dreams*.

In two instances, dancing appears as the real-life event on
which the dream draws: in one, where Freud attempts to
explain "embarrassing dreams of being naked," arguing that
these dreams always relate to childhood memories, he gives the
example of one patient who could connect such a dream to a
memory of wanting to dance into his sister's room in a night-
shirt; in another, "A Chemist's Dream," dreamt by a young man
who was "endeavouring to give up his habit of masturbating in
favour of sexual relations with women," the dreamer realizes in
analysis that his dream refers to a woman whom, in waking life,
he had "clasped to himself" too tightly during a dancing lesson

the night before, leading to a dream wherein he "substituted himself for the magnesium" in a solution he was supposed to be making, and then "found himself in a singularly unstable state," which, as Freud describes it, seems intentional. His legs go weak, he dissolves, he pulls himself out of the "vessel" in which he's making the phenyl-magnesium-bromide, he announces "it's working," he wakes up to remember to tell this dream to Freud, falls back asleep, and dreams that he misses an appointment to meet a woman by oversleeping.[18]

Neither dreamer dreams *of* dancing, though; instead, IRL dancing leads them to dream. When Hamilton was a teenager, in years formative for her ideas about love and friendship, she listened to a song, "In Dreams I Dance with You." The song's lyrics are silly: "In my bed at night I dream you're a ghost / That only cats can see," for example. But as in Hamilton's dreams, in this song, the dancing is a respite from a stressful context: the speaker dances with his addressee "while murderers and rapists surround the house," but they "don't care;" it's not possible for the dream to be stressful when it involves this dancing.

The above evidence suggests that people do not dance in *The Interpretation of Dreams* because those who are so lucky to dance asleep do not need to bring their dreams for analysis. Their dancing protects them.

Like perverts, dancers are unusually satisfied.

Something changes, though.

One day, Hamilton dreams that she is sending an email to Connor that is a picture of the whiteboard in her bedroom; it has a list (typically a to-do list would appear on this board) that begins "I miss you" and ends with "I'm lonely."

---

[18] Freud, *Interpretation*, xxx.

Instead of sending it to Connor, she accidentally emails it to all of her colleagues. To deal with her embarrassment, she decides to go on a first date with a stranger, perhaps to renew her confidence, a man who tells her he is very good at reviving plants. When Hamilton describes the sorry state of her boss's office plant, he convinces her to give it to him to fix. But he takes the plant into a store, where he ghosts—he never emerges from the store or returns any of her calls—and Hamilton is forced to inform her boss, the same week she has emailed everyone the whiteboard informing Connor she misses her, that she has given her plant away to a man she hardly knew.

After this second embarrassment, she goes to a poetry reading and sits on the floor, where her ex puts his arm around her body. She yells: "I don't talk to you, what makes you think you can touch me?" He accuses her of overreacting. She overreacts more. He says "not this again," calls her melodramatic, and her friends look on.

This dream ended altogether the nightly dreams of dancing with Connor.

At the time of this recording, Hamilton was not aware that Connor is excellent at caring for and maintaining plant life.

*

This is about dreams and writing
them down. There's a fake "neutrality"
though: if "who's dreaming?" affects dream content,
it matters who gets to sleep through the night,

as implied by the title of Rindon Johnson's
Nobody Sleeps Better than White People,
which is also a line in the book's first poem, "Mom Look":

> Johnson, Rindon. Excerpt from "Mom Look." *Nobody Sleeps Better than White People*.

> Mom Look,
> Nobody sleeps better than white people.

> They cuff us to hospital beds and then go home and sleep.

> Anything can be a hospital bed, mom.

> Fuck us is what they're saying, mom.

> I'll cuss if I want to, mom.

> It doesn't matter how many women raise their hands at a funeral—
> the clouds are getting thick here—I'm just a black man, mom.

> You used to rub my back so I could go to sleep but you're too tall
> for me to rub yours.[19]

---

[19] Rindon Johnson, *Nobody Sleeps Better Than White People* (Brooklyn, NY: Inpatient Press, 2016).

I wrote a presumptuous email to Rin about sleeping:

Hamilton, Diana. Email to Rindon Johnson, November 21, 2016.

Since I sent you the picture of your book overlapping with the Guardian article[20] on white women sleeping well, I have been trying to learn more about who goes to sleep.

I am writing a poem that is making an argument, perhaps you have seen it—the argument is that dreaming is writing. (You appear in it, I just realized, I took one of your dreams about your mom). Many of the dreams in it, the ones that are my dreams, are about being a writer, or being at a party with writers, or wanting to write, etc. Do you have dreams about being a poet, and are they stressful?

Now that I am learning about who goes to sleep, I am also learning that perhaps white people have the most dreams. I am also trying to learn whether every dream in Freud's *The Interpretation of Dreams*, for example, is a white person's dream.

Now, I am reading a racist article from *Psychology Today*,[21] arguing that a preference for 'lightness' is a 'universal archetype' and the cause of racism rather than its result. It uses dreams as evidence for this claim.

Johnson did not respond then, but they did later:

---

[20] Arwa Mahdawi, "How a Good Night's Sleep Became the Ultimate Status Symbol," *The Guardian*, June 1 2016, https://www.theguardian.com/lifeand-style/2016/jun/01/sleep-habits-eight-hours-health-wellness-arianna-huffington

[21] Jeremy Taylor, "Dreaming, Racism, and the Unconscious," *Psychology Today*, https://www.psychologytoday.com/blog/the-wisdom-your-dreams/201010/dreaming-racism-and-the-unconscious

Johnson, Rindon. "Email to Diana Hamilton," September 22, 2017.

I don't dream about being a poet, I did not expect to be one and don't really self identify; I'm a disassociating poet if anything, I guess even people who disassociate have dreams, but I don't really dream and when I do the world is ending or something and when I wake up it still is. So my dreams are realistic I guess.

A UCSD study found a "black-white
sleep gap" and a UChicago study showed
"Whites, women and wealthy sleep longer, better."[22]

White women dream 6.7 hours a night, white men dream 6.1 hours, black women dream 5.9 hours, and black men dream 5.1 hours.

*

[22] Mahdawi, "Good Night's Sleep," *The Guardian*.

In *Psychopathic Characters on the Stage*,
Freud discusses the "preconditions for enjoyment"
to which creative writing is subject:

> Lyric poetry serves the purpose, more than anything, of giving
> vent to intense feelings of many sorts—just as was at one time
> the case with dancing.[23]

Lyric poetry must have been more exciting in 1906.

In the case of the man who presses his nethers too
forcefully against his dance partner, clasping her
waist in a way that forces her to cry out, he struggles
against his inability to "give vent" now that masturbation
has been taken off the table. Men do this, perhaps others:
they quit masturbating, and they dream
differently in response. A virulent misogynist
once gave a poetry reading—rather, this happens
all the time, but—once, one prefaced it
by saying he had quit masturbating
for a month to see how it changed his dreams, resulting
in his poems. I did not believe him: he made it sound
like his dreams went to private school
and then studied abroad in Paris, where they sexually assaulted
women about whose clavicles the young poet dreamt:

---

[23] Sigmund Freud, "Psychopathic Characters on the Stage," in *Writing on Art and
Literature*, ed. by Werner Hamacher and David E. Wellbery (California: Stan-
ford University Press, 1997), 88.

minivanman1, "r/NoFap," *reddit*, 2016.

On the subreddit community for men who come together around the decision to abstain from masturbation (some have already made this commitment, others are there to learn more), minivanman1 offers, "Are you starting to have vivid dreams? Congrats, your dopaminergic reward pathways are healing!"

Many men are shocked to learn that their heretofore lack of dreams could have been caused by regular masturbation:

> This is a revelation to me. My sister has so many dreams and last week, I remember, I told her I almost never have dreams. Now I know this is also related to fap . . . Incredible how it messes up our basic functions. I really need to stop this disgusting habit!

This user does not indicate whether he asked his sister if she also abstains.

Others chime in to say that, though they've given up this par-ticular dream-killer, they smoke weed, which this forum agrees also takes away your dreams (and, some report with sadness, pot makes one's penis "whisper in one's ear," a slippery slope as they say).

It's hard to argue for laziness
by providing evidence of laziness's productivity
without undoing the original claim:
It's hard to argue for laziness
because you'll be tempted to "perform it"
by arguing lazily. If dreaming is writing
but coming and smoking prevent dreaming
but dreaming, writing, coming, and being high
are all good, what do you choose? Don't
trust an argument that asks you to.

Freud, Sigmund, "A Modified Staircase Dream," *The Interpretation of Dreams.*

One of my patients, a man whose sexual abstinence was imposed on him by a severe neurosis, and whose phantasies were fixed upon his mother, had repeated dreams of going upstairs in her company. I once remarked to him that a moderate amount of masturbation would probably do him less harm than his compulsive self-restraint, and this provoked the following dream:

His piano-teacher reproached him for neglecting his piano-playing, and for not practising Mocheles' 'Etudes' and Clementi's 'Gradus ad Parnassum.'

By way of comment, he pointed out that 'Gradus' are also 'steps'; and that the key-board itself is a staircase, since it contains scales.

It is fair to say that there is no group of ideas that is incapable of representing sexual facts and wishes.

Freud does not identify what quantity of masturbation is "moderate," nor, if the *études* for neurosis are masturbation, how to study for dreams.

*

I won't lean on Freud
to argue that dreams write:
anyone for whom his arguments function
as evidence already believes too much in words.
"The unconscious is structured like a language;" the Talmud
and *Die Traumdeutung* both focus on wordplay and puns
in understanding dreams, Freud complains about translation, etc.
This is why, some say, Freud disliked the movies:

> Michel, Régis. "Dumme Dinge: Freud cinéphobe?" *Savoirs et clinique: Freud et l'image* 1/2010 (n° 12), 58-68.

The English translation of this title has no silly things, no cinéphobe to answer the question it implies: "Considering Freud's Views on Cinema." The abstract claims that Freud "must deny the cinema, which is the opposite (the rival of) dreams":

> . . . the cinema stole from Freud the most precious thing, the material, even, of his art: the image . . . *The Interpretation of Dreams* is really . . . purely narrative. It deals with nothing but stories. Not images. The text is made of dreams. But a dream is a story, where the image is second, language first.[24]

The cinema is a dream-thief, but its theft is a misreading.

*

---

[24] Régis Michel, "Dumme Dinge: Freud cinéphobe?" Translation mine.

43

My dreams aren't often about words:
they're about an attempted motion
or the sound of water or being observed or getting caught
out in desire or being unable to maintain control
of a car moving too quickly or being saved
from a disaster or being misunderstood or
the embarrassment of wanting to be a good writer
or a good friend or a good daughter or a hot person.

Except the "I love you" dreams, dating from early 2016,
beginning with the aforementioned dream of signing
a book with said confession, leading to a series
of at least twenty dreams, all hinging on
whether "I love you" will be or has been said, often dreamt
in bed beside a lover who woke up, eyes open, to say it
all the time, with conviction, but who didn't know
about & slept through these nocturnal emissions:

Hamilton, Diana. "I love you dream." Date unknown.

Hamilton sees that D has left his checking account statement out
for her to find. She knows it is a message to her. At the bottom,
it reads: ATM PIN: L-O-V-E

She wakes up, texts D the dream. He responds that, having
transcribed his actual PIN to letters via the keypad, he learns
she's just one off:

it's "L-O-Q-E." She knows that he and her dream would like her
to know that he is only one letter off from loving her.

*

Michel doesn't find "proof" of Freud's disdain
in his published work, but in a letter home:

Freud, Sigmund. Letter "to the family," September 21, 1907.

. . . the boredom is interrupted by short cinematographic
performances for the sake of which the old children (your
father included) suffer quietly the advertisements and
monotonous photographs. They are stingy with the tidbits,
however, so I have had to look at the same thing over and
over again. When I turn to go I detect a certain tension in
the crowd, which makes me look again, and sure enough a
new performance has begun, and so I stay on. Until 9PM I
usually remain spellbound; then I begin to feel too lonely in
the crowd, so I return to my room to write to you all after
having ordered a bottle of fresh water.

Freud's at the Piazza Colonna watching lantern-slides, lamenting
to his family how this childish entertainment sucks him in.

That's his complaint: not that the mélange of images contradicts
dream logic, but that it's both too addictive and too banal. This
is the feeling of binge-watching TV, where the relief of an ad's
ending, the recognition a cliffhanger is coming, and a curiosity
about what one's friends are watching, all conspire to create a
system of intermittent reward that precludes the question of
whether the show itself is pleasurable.

If Freud lamented film, film theory liked psychoanalysis.

When you like something, you hope it likes you back.

Even if your crush isn't returned, you hope be thought of—to be disliked is at least kind of care—rather than ignored. So scholars look for evidence of his disdain, in the absence of any other attention: that though filmmakers claim to give us some access to dreams, they have no idea how dreams operate—or that films don't rely on the linguistic structure of the unconscious—or anything more theoretically important than boredom at the piazza.

Instead, Freud's a snob who feels guilty for having been entertained.

Well, he's not *just* a snob: he's also a tourist voyeur of racist footage:

Marcus, Laura. "Dreaming and Cinematographic Consciousness."

Marcus reads Freud's letter to his family by noting his lack of interest in relaying the projections' "content." Instead, he describes the experience of "looking again," of being called on to rewatch: "The spellbinding nature of the spectacle," she concludes, "is precisely the display of its own visibility."[25]

But Marcus is just as disinterested in the images' content as Freud. The lantern slides are

> actually advertisements, but to beguile the public these are interspersed with pictures of landscapes, Negroes of the Congo, glacier ascents, and so on

Freud's letter specifies. Marcus ignores what these images are, because, she insists, the scene is about looking itself rather than about what we look at.

*

[25] Laura Marcus, "Dreaming and Cinematic Consciousness," *The Dreams of Interpretation: A Century Down the Royal Road*, ed. Catherine Lieu (Minneapolis: University of Minnesota Press, 2007), 197-214.

I dream about "love" for a year.

Finally, I get to dream about love itself,
rather than the word, and in Paris, of all places: a place of movies
and of dreams, a place that is not real, or at least, that's best
enjoyed as unreal (in the real Paris, the *gendarmes*
have machine guns). I dreamt that a cat appeared
between us in bed where the only thing missing,
perhaps, were the cat that normally gives us a location
for the expression of both love and "love." "I love you," we say
to each other's cats, only to each other
in or around dreams. In the dream, for a moment, I was lucid:
I knew I was dreaming that we were asleep in bed.

Because I knew this, I summoned a cat.

When the cat appeared, I lost my lucidity
and believed the cat to be real: it was grey,
it was sleeping right in the center
of the covers, and it had a shimmering green
effect on its fur on the top of its head and down
its back (much like the green of a mallard duck or a pigeon,
which they identify with, believing that
I have implied many times over that they are useless
and beautiful, like a male bird) (in identifying with that duck,
they imply that I am dull grey, tasked with work). But this cat was two
sexes, in bird norms: dull grey and shimmering
green, useful and lazy; it combined us
and gave us a place to put love. They explained, in the dream,
that this is a common effect called "goldenrod"
that can happen to all creatures.

I woke up, but not entirely: I lived
much of the morning in this half-awake state,
which is to say that I became very afraid. I knew
these were not the right dreams for saying goodbye.

As with an old therapist, three sessions to go, expensive
but an "emergency" created by heartbreak: and yet I came
in with the kinds of conversations, she pointed out,
that one has with a therapist one expects to see for years
(I just described my dreams).

I couldn't have a conversation that acknowledged the "end."

I fell back asleep, but not all the way, to see everything
as a landscape: I said aloud, "I wish we were in the mountains."
I saw them, generically: mountains, ocean, field, animals
arranged; I remembered a friend's work on the relationship
between idealized natural landscapes and moral and aesthetic
philosophy; I realized I had chosen an idealized landscape
(cue footage of the Luxembourg gardens) in order to make a scene
for this non-ideal conversation, the end; the landscape doesn't
know how to end either, or it does too well. I wanted to
cry. I needed to dream of love's environs, not its words.

I wondered, or at least believed, that if I held the trees in mind
long enough, I would figure out not only what love I might have
but also how to quit my job and my sadness
and other drudgeries, everything seemed to be held
in the image of trees, I feared
that I would become a romantic poet or, worse, a poet
who substitutes birds names for the specific contexts
of their loves, their lives, etc., I didn't want to wake up,
I thought all of this belonged perhaps in the dream poem,
which is about love, perhaps in the poem about animals,
which is about what goes wrong when we try to understand
ourselves through creatures, perhaps in the story

about dealing with anxiety by watching movies,
I'd rewatch *Casablanca* for it, "We'll always have Paris,"
these books are all the same, trying
to answer the question of what leads someone who imagines
anything, say, a sky or a character, to believe
that, by imagining, and by writing
what was imagined down,
they'll answer a hard question.

*

Freud may not prove that dreaming is writing, but
Die Traumdeutung is an archive, you can't deny
that the dreams take up space on the pages, indicating that,
with enough sleep, you'll have a book-length manuscript.

I'm curious about masturbation
as baby steps, though: do you think Freud's patient got off
before he dreamt he should practice his *études*,
or does the dream merely echo F's reproach?

"I have not come in seven days,"
I started to write, and then remembered, no,
that isn't true, I have not entirely neglected
my piano-playing, and the only dream I recall
this week followed said lesson:

> Hamilton, Diana. "Dream before leaving for Kentucky." January
>   2017.

> Hamilton walks out of a window and onto a dock, but a dock
> without water below it, a fire escape, in fact, made of wood that
> stays in place without stairs or other support.

> At first, the deck seems to operate via some sort of pulley system,
> and when she steps out of the window, she tries to lower it, but
> does it wrong. An ex comes out the same window and begins to
> explain how she has erred, but in the end, they demonstrate that
> they can make it levitate such that they are now floating while
> having a fight.

> They tell her that she has always been difficult, as they float on
> the deck, and she gets very sad. She decides that the only way to
> not get more depressed in response is to go for a run.

Despite the difficulty of running in dreams, Hamilton does it; she even manages to run fast instead of encountering the normal underwater-dream-resistance. She runs to Deming Park, the park of her childhood, where she often runs in her dreams but never ran growing up. She looks down and finds out she is barefoot, which she hadn't noticed because she had been levitating, and she sees she is also holding a pile of laundry and dropping the clothes as she runs. She returns to the house and is proud to note she has run "two miles."

We have to get our priorities in order.

I want to dream, I don't want to go to work,
I want to sleep, I don't want to check my email,
I want to fly over a pond of koi fish, the word
"coy" echoing off water and clouds, I don't want to
create a personal budget. But those who love to dream
can become assholes, it's like you're demanding
a personal TV series that no one else is allowed to watch
and which the entirety of your day is organized around viewing.

I searched my dream journals for a transition, here:
a dream that related to masturbation, to dancing, to crushes,
to restraint, to abstinence, to love, to friendship. I found,
instead, an interruption—a complaint that "life"
came between my dreams, instead of another dream.

There's more than one interrupted dream
in *Venus and Furs*: when Wanda instructs Apollo
to whip Severin, "Apollo whipped all poetry
from" him and he realizes he's been caught in the "net
of woman's treachery" "as though [he] were awakening
from a long dream." In this unconvincing resolution,
Severin loses his interest in the Venus in Furs,
making a dual call for women's subjection and their rights:

The moral is that woman, as Nature created her and as man up to now as found her attractive, is man's enemy; she can be his slave or his mistress but never his companion. This she can only be when she has the same rights as he and is his equal in education and work. For the time being there is only one alternative: to be the hammer or the anvil.[26]

Between the opening and closing dreams
of *Venus in Furs*, Severin's dreams come unhappily true.

Between my dreams, I complain
about the world's intervention:

> Hamilton, Diana. "Dream of Inconvenient Shower." November 16, 2013.

Hamilton is with an ex's parents and has to shower, but their shower is in the center of the room without drain, curtains, or glass; just a showerhead over the carpeted floor in a shared social space. She has to solve this problem (a recurring one). In the journal, she notes that she also has an issue with the shampoo, and that she paid for something in cookies.

Then, she writes:

> X wants a hug (real life) so I feel not left alone to do my thinking

and notes that she woke up "so much more alert than usual."

A girl so respects her dream life
that a lover's need to hug her while she sleeps
not only disrespects her "thinking" but also
merits transcription.

---

[26] Deleuze, *Masochism*, 271.

Meanwhile, the important thinking she's doing
in her sleep is all about cookies:

Ibid.

I was buying cookies at a cookie store and lost my wallet. I found
it. I never got to eat the cookies.

Three years and two months later, she dreamt again:

---. Email, January 19, 2017.

The writer has lunch with either X, with whom she was living,
or with current lover, or with both, or perhaps with many exes at
once, purportedly in order to look at a map.

Rather, it is a smaller subset of a larger map, and the writer knows
that the larger map is at her home—"a map of something else."

She decides to run to her own apartment (implying she does not,
in fact, live with any of these exes with whom she is dining) to
retrieve it (Hamilton developed the ability to run in her dreams
in 2016). Once she has gotten a block or so, though, she realizes
it would take "one hour and a half to get the map and return."

Instead, she runs back, passing a sidewalk café where, she sees
now, she left her wallet and cigarettes, a table since abandoned
by the ex(es). She narrates all this in the "voice memos" function
of her phone.

In the recording, she tries to remember: "What was the thing I
said?" she asks. A long pause, a groan. "It had to do with listening
to his radio show."

You lose your wallet looking for cookies.

You find your wallet, you miss your cookies, you lose your wallet

looking for maps. You find your wallet, miss maps, you're interrupted

by your impression of men's need

for your attention, you lose their attention, you find men

to miss you, you overlook the fact that the need, and the attention,

were yours to begin with. Call yourself on the phone, girl.

*

Someone asked the internet,

"Does anyone know the meaning of slow dancing (in a dream)?"

and describes a dream of dancing with her crush.

Someone answers:

"It means you want to slow dance with your crush."

Mayer recommends "borrowing a friend's
dreams." Robert Glück takes this further. His book,
About Ed, which is about Ed Aulerich-Sugai, a former
lover, whom Glück describes as "a Japanese-American artist . . .
a sexual mountain climber, a real explorer. Also
he was a great dreamer," isn't done, but it borrows
many of Ed's dreams, according to interviews,
according to Glück, according to my memory of Glück
reading at the Poetry Project on 12/7/2016
(I had the uncommon pleasure of turning 31 at midnight, crying,
outside of the Cock, across which I had danced with Stacy,
before she left, before I cried, unrelated to the dancing
or to the reading, and where I had not introduced
myself to Bob, and where I was recovering from a different crying,
the crying related to *About Ed*, from which I would guess
he read the second section, about Ed's "illness, his death,
[Bob's] mourning"—this is Glück's
"version of an AIDs memoir except it's a novel."

He spoke, albeit briefly, about getting Ed
to dream for him, about (or perhaps my notes translated
it this way, I can't tell) a sort of laziness: if to dream is to write,

meaning we can write by sleeping, how much dreamier
to have someone else dream for us, to let our sleep be
unproductive and to trust our writing is being written
by ex-lovers, in the past, in their dream journals.
Borrowing is not the right word: he cannot give these dreams back.
Instead, he can give them to his novel; in an interview, he explains
that Ed's dreams will make up the weather:

Leuzzi, Tony. From "Interview with Robert Glück," *EOAGH*,
  Oct. 23, 2011.

So, you have been collaborating with Ed for a long time!

We were artists together. He would draw me, I would write
poems about our relationship, first how good it was, then how
fucked up. I plan to make all the weather in the book come from
his dreams. He was always watching the sky and painting the sky
and so I think it will be good to have all the atmosphere come
from his dreams.

If you struggle to keep dream journals
for yourself, keep them instead for a writer, a friend, a date,
someone lovely enough to collaborate with you
in your death, while they find out, via collaboration,
whether they are willing to survive you:

Now I recall last night's dream—that I am the one moving out,
and there is Ed, helping me paint my huge multi-storied loft,
and also undertaking such projects as locating a copper bath tub.
Denny is in the dream too, he just got a dog who is entirely
unruly, and Denny holds him back with his I-know-I'm-in-the-
wrong amused expression. Now I understand the dream means
that Ed was giving me a hand with this book—this project in
which we separate a third time. In the dream he wore the body
I slept with for eight years, except when he was sleeping with
someone else.[27]

Today, I reread an article I first read 10 years ago: D.W. Winnicott's "Transitional Objects and Transitional Phenomena:"

> As the infant starts to use organized sounds ('mum', 'ta', 'da') there may appear a 'word' for the transitional object. The name given by the infant to these earliest objects is often significant, and it usually has a word used by the adults partly incorporated in it. For instance, 'baa' may be the name, and the 'b' may have come from the adult's use of the word 'baby' or 'bear'.[28]

I read this the first time because I had made a blanket.

I crocheted the blanket because a woman was pregnant.

One reason otherwise nice girls get into psychoanalysis,
I think, is that, in learning to seem serious to your teachers
you must learn not to "relate" "personally" to the text, if
you're savvy and see this early difference between As and Bs,
for example, and while, with psychoanalysis, the demand
to not relate is even greater in a seminar context, it's impossible
at the level of reading: if you had such an object, and you read
this quote, you are now thinking of its name.
"Mimi" was named, "me, me," the thing I shouted whenever
someone tried to take the blanket away, and almost a record
of my stutter: my robotic doll, programmed to cry "mama"
when squeezed, broke, such that she cried
"mmm-mm-mm-aaa-mmmaa-maaaa," I thought she mocked me:

The woman who was pregnant was my professor: this was important,
because she also took me Seriously. She paid me $10
an hour to go to the library and read books &
watch Kiarostami movies. "I'm writing a paper

[27] Robert Glück, from "About Ed," *Belladonna Elders Series #2* (New York: Belladonna, 2008), 20.

[28] D.W. Winnicott, "Transitional Objects and Transitional Phenomena," *International Journal of Psycho-Analysis* 34 (1953), 89-97.

on the relationship between the camera
and the gun, Diana, would you go to the library
and find some articles on this subject?" As evidence
that this was a Good Mentor I offer the fact that, when
I graduated, she gave me a raise to $15/hour without my asking.

(Not only was this the best job I've had, she's also the only professor
kind enough to have tried to talk me out of grad school.)

This was the first time someone I so admired
was going to have a baby. I bought the most expensive blue
yarn I could afford; it was a very soft blanket
that probably cost, in materials, six hours of labor
paid by its recipient, plus the 50-or-so unpaid hours
of construction. I was proud. I handed
it to her. She seemed, more than anything, confused.

"Did you make this?" she asked. I said yes, happily. She told me
that students do not typically knit baby blankets for their professors.

Embarrassed, I tried to explain:
I told her about my own Mimi, how important
my blanket was to me, that I could not have lived
without it, that it seemed to have mattered
when I learned someone made it with their hands,
this blanket was everything, I said, when I imagined
what a baby needed, I imagined a crocheted blanket.

The professor was unwilling to let me become a caretaker;
she needed me to return to my position as student.

"Oh," she said. "Have you read Winnicott on transitional objects?"

*

Fear and Trembling

Fear and Trembling

Elsie Maria Kingdon

[I found this novella—if you can call it that—on Christmas Eve, 2016, outside of Metrograph, a movie theater in lower Manhattan. I was coming from a screening of Carol, *the adaptation of Patricia Highsmith's lesbian classic,* The Price of Salt. *I asked at the theater and the neighboring bars to try to track down its writer, and I performed the requisite searches, but she's either made use of a pseudonym or written in relative obscurity (of course, coming advances in machine learning will make identifying her easier). Though, lying in the gutter, it gave the impression of having fallen out of a taxi in some sort of skirmish, the manuscript looked freshly printed, and had the phrase "FINAL DRAFT" as a running header. —D.S.H.]*

Recently, every young person I know agreed they were "very anxious."

Life was full of dread, they said, and the body, they discovered, warded off problems by creating "meaningful," if unhelpful, physical symptoms.

They started acting as if knowing this served some purpose, as if, to recover from anxiety, it were enough to recognize it.

Their parents having loved them too much or too little, their shits, cum, coughs, and dizzy spells, their sleeping too much, their forgetting the purpose in going to work or going for walks, their feelings of sadness and difficulty making decisions, their desire to sleep with abusers or fathers (that too-often inclusive 'or')—all these were not only signs of some hopefully identifiable pathology, but necessary steps.

They could not say towards what, precisely, but they seemed to imagine they were inching closer to a successfully repressive adulthood, towards their careers, or, I don't fucking know, towards Connecticut.

Laura looked forward to telling her future children about the time she believed she was dying from watching *Avatar 3D*, from the plot's stupid allegory, the apparent proximity of weird shapes to her face, and the two cups of coffee she had before the show—all combining to produce heart palpitations, tears, and the sense that she would never be allowed to leave the theater. When she does tell her kids this, one day, she will make it into an "incident," safe in its isolation; she will forget, consciously or un-, how she couldn't go to the movies for a year.

I know: Like all anxious people before them, they have suffered. Some still suffer, stubbornly; for these, the symptoms are signs only of sadness's truth. These I admire more—though they're worse off—than those who recover quickly: those who shat blood or fell flat on the sidewalk, bed, or veranda in order to "move on," and who did move on, though only in a limited sense: their bowels regained consistency as unhappy couples do (by deciding to get married to solve their problems). The binding removes only the outward sign that there is something to deal with.

The girl who stands up from her collapse in order to recover never bothers to wonder how she got there, or why, or what this terror meant, outside of a general narrative of self-improvement—she devotes herself to a set of tasks meant to produce recovery without reflection, with the post-religious zeal of a lapsed Catholic.

Instead of getting up and, whatever, "going running," she should stay on the sidewalk where she fainted. (If she has, at this point in the story, already stood up, it is time to lie back down.) She could not be expected to do this all day, of course— that would be dull—but whenever she starts to forget that it's impossible to stay upright, she should talk to strangers while prone, if she can bring herself to, or let herself be talked at. Cities could provide funding for such programs in order to stem the tide of productivity currently ruining the potential for new friendships and affairs, both of which are known to stimulate local economies.

Though Laura will deny herself this knowledge in her future, she had it then, or now: after avoiding the movies, after trying to get "better" by reading "books" and "taking it easy," she tried attending as many as possible.

She took notes on her anxiety's progress: "Gripping the torn-up upholstery on the armrests at Film Forum while the newly restored edition of Fritz Lang's *Metropolis* plays," she wrote, "I might vomit or worse," the worse being her belief that the film would never end.

(As the armrests at Film Forum are actually intact, this is further evidence that the theater had become a hard drive for her fears. Laura was a bad writer, and like other bad writers, she asked description to stand in for feeling.)

At the same time, though, she was happy: unlike with the

first film-induced panic attack, this movie was great. It was worth freaking out through. She noted how contemporary special effects had inscribed themselves so successfully on her body that an identical reaction could now be triggered by sharp lighting contrasts in a 1927 silent film: the longer shots were tied to the stress produced by the awful brevity that had so specifically gotten under her eyelids before.

Realizing she could more easily leave this time, having attended alone, she didn't mind staying. Going alone removed this factor—the fear that, if she were to become anxious, she would to have to make an awkward exit from a date, for example—and made the anticipation of panic more experimental ("If I choose a relaxed posture, do I calm down? Do I pay more or less attention when I'm anxious? Does attraction to one of the actors make it easier?"). In a week where she had passed out daily on the way to work, she went to see *Carol* for the second time, having guessed that the presence of friends at the first screening had prevented the escape she needed, via the movie's textiles. The train-panic rose into her throat, but in the theater, she was guaranteed a seat; she considered thanking God for this comfort, remembered she didn't believe in him, and thanked the seat itself; she started to cry, exhausted from how hard she had had to work to stay calm that year, and realized everyone else was crying too, but about Therese's impossible love; she joined them; she imagined her hands in the folds of Carol's fur; she gasped aloud at how heartbroken she was to not yet have had the love of a woman; she sank back into the seat; she stayed on edge, but every edge had another scene beyond it.

In movies, from there on, she did not find relief from her stress, per se, but she found a place to keep it. The scenes that made her panic in each film became related, so that her symptoms proved themselves able to write a new movie out of their overlaps.

Films teach us this need for a repetition unachievable in our less cinematic moments. Anxiety should not be avoided, they tell us, and fainting women should stay on the ground. We see this especially in George Cukor's 1949 film *Adam's Rib*, which isn't even a movie about stress, but about love.

Adam and Amanda Bonner, in addition to being married, are lawyers on opposing sides of a case against Doris, a woman who shot her husband out of jealousy after finding him in another's arms. Amanda defends her in order to protest the double standard applied to men and women accused of the same crime. Adam, a shitty man, takes the side of the husband and the law.

The situation comes to a head when Amanda humiliates her husband during the trial, directing one of her female witnesses, a prize-winning weightlifter, to pick Adam up and throw him over her shoulder. The weightlifter is only one of many women she calls to serve as character witnesses, not on behalf of the defendant, but of femininity as such. Amanda's insistence on the case's relationship to gender—and, more pointedly, the way she makes him look foolish in the courtroom—later drives Adam to storm out of the house. When the verdict comes in, Amanda's plea to the jury to "judge this case as you would if the sexes were reversed" proves successful, and the defendant is found not guilty.

But this is not the point, yet, where we learn about anxiety; it's simply an excellent plot. In addition to the lady-scientists and lady-bodybuilders called to the stand, the defense questions the "other woman," at whom the defendant shot before shooting her husband. She testifies how she began to "conk out" after hearing the gunshots—"Everything went black"—and then fainted in the hallway.

Finally, we have the fainting woman we wanted: but will she respond to smelling salts and carry on, or will she stay on the ground?

It's the wrong question, as a careful viewer knows she never fainted. Her testimony is made unreliable in two ways—first, in Amanda's line of questioning:

Defense:	Everything went black a little earlier, didn't it, Miss Cain?
Cain:	What?
Defense:	I refer to the color of the black silk negligee you put on to receive Mr. Attinger.

The fainting is a literal cover-up, made of silk.

Second, and more tellingly, the viewer has at this point already seen the shooting in the opening sequence, where no fainting occurs. The only thing that fades to black is the camera, as the shot transitions from the defendant holding her injured husband to a headline reporting the crime. The camera loses its sight and sound, as it so often does, but we see Miss Cain very much on her feet.

In doing so, she sets a great example: rather than attempting to move on from an earlier nervous spell that would have threatened to limit her self-control in the future, she invents symptoms she actually failed to produce. Better still, she ensures the attack is recorded by the court stenographer, to be repeated on request.

Today, though, young people aren't content to be anxious wrecks; they go right on. They go to work, especially, or to death, or to drink. You can tell they think it's something to move past in how often it happens on their commutes: if they confine their anxiety to a specific vehicle, they can leave it in the glove compartment or the second car; they think a panic attack is a mode of transportation to a restorative yoga class offered on a sliding scale in their interestingly diverse neighborhoods.

Unlike the express train, though, anxiety always comes on time.

— It's coming, someone observes.

— But it's already come! Her friend admonishes.

— I have to get ready, she adds.

— We've had this conversation before, her friend suggests.

— I have to sit down, she insists.

— We've barely started our walk, her friend objects.

— If I were an animal, some specific animal whose qualities I admire, then I could maybe . . .

— You wouldn't feel this way if you were that animal, her friend interrupts.

— You can't know that. If I were the animal, or even a man . . .

— Let's not go there, the friend sighs.

— I'm not going anywhere. I am sitting right here, she realizes.

— You've got to pull it together, her friend notes.

— You used to be better at helping me with this, she complains.

— I didn't know I'd have to help you for fucking ever, her friend clarifies.

Return to Spencer Tracy (as Adam) and Katherine Hepburn (as his Rib). Remember that we are not in what some see as the original love story—although surely there's something to be learned from *that* couple's transition from ease to a life-long nervous condition, especially given life's then-greater length, "as it is written."

We are not even, anymore, watching Cukor's film, although I wish we were—instead, we are reading Stanley Cavell's imagining of this Adam in *Pursuits of Happiness*, his readings of the Hollywood "remarriage plot."

In *Adam's Rib*, as in many remarriage plots, the source of the couple's unhappiness is the woman's employment. Throughout, Adam assumes he would be better off if his wife were not also a lawyer; here, we have additional confirmation that that avoiding anxiety is essentially retrogressive.

The way Cavell watches this movie, he sees Tracy-as-Adam sitting in the courtroom, knowing his love for his wife obliges some interference in the prosecution of Doris, another wife, but also knowing the law. The camera suggests he will experience some reprieve, as the shot stays close to the witness.

But when Doris describes catching her husband in the act, the camera turns to the courtroom's audience, as if looking for something. It fails to find anything to land on. During this pause, Adam realizes he's supposed to object.

Cavell describes how this camera movement produces an unidentifiable anxiety that becomes clear only *after* he objects: he was "failing for a few difficult moments to pick up his cue," since the testimony had clearly stopped for *something*, and the camera finds only his silence. This is when "we find words for our anxiety." The words we find, though, suggest only that our anxiety is the same as Tracy's: we cannot find our words at first, and find them only by realizing he can't find his.

This is not a feeling to be "worked through." Should Adam, in consultation with his Cognitive-Behavioral Therapist, reconsider how his thoughts and actions resulted in this anxiety? He could reconstruct his attitude towards this case by breaking it into three new thoughts:

Thought #1: This case presents an interesting challenge. I love the opportunity to address both my relationship and my profession head-on! (Happy, Excited)

Thought #2: Perhaps, given the overlap between my love for my wife and my love for justice, I should back out of this case. Someone else might be better qualified to approach it objectively. (Neutral)

Thought #3: I am a terrible fucking lawyer. Everyone will see me hesitate to take a firm stance. (Anxious, Sad)

Through this cognitive restructuring process, might he use this scene as a learning opportunity to identify a pattern of negative thoughts that could be consciously replaced with more useful thoughts? Or should he recount his feelings during this scene while his eyes rapidly track a therapist's hands, uncovering earlier unresolved memories? Should he lie horizontal, wait for the silence to pass, wonder whether his interlocutor is either gay or attractive, think about the way he felt hiding under the covers as a child, hope for a different future feeling? He doesn't need to. His future has a very specific length determined by the final cut of the film.

Of course, the question for Adam is not whether he will win, but whether his relationship will survive. And as it is firmly in the tradition of the remarriage plot, the audience need not suffer another parallel anxiety; they can happily take for granted both the divorce and the reunion. Of interest is only the banter that pushes love along.

Banter's necessity returns us to the courtroom's awkward silence. This is what anxiety is: a speaker's block, a stutter. We know it will take words to make love, but what if we don't find them? Someone watches us wonder this. It is hopeless. We lose interest in activities that used to give us pleasure. If we do manage to speak—which, despite ourselves, we often do—what comes out is awful, and we replay what we said later, in solitude, to identify just what slips provide the best justification for self-harm.

Adam must speak to judge, jury, wife, and viewer, and he largely succeeds at doing so; only a viewer as obsessive as a philosopher would identify the "pause" before his objection as sustained enough to provoke anxiety. Even worse, it would seem, Adam is nothing but a character, confined only to those scenes in which he appears, barring those that were cut. There is no hope for words beyond those written for him, and his anxiety, such as it is, is caused not by negative thoughts, but by the camera's direction.

How does he learn that he does not have the words, then?

In submitting to the constraints of a script, he is given the opportunity to see himself repeated.

Tracy-as-Adam, I mean, is *lucky* to be fictional.

If only my friends didn't exist either.

Each time we have a drink, I listen to their "new" problems, and I become surer that their real problem is their belief that they're in control. They remain under the impression that they (with the help of advice and red wine) should learn to quit having these thoughts, and that there's something they should do to make positive changes in their lives. They relive already-written scripts just as Spencer Tracy does, but they act as though they have agency mid-scene.

Many anxious people today could do better to see themselves as situated in advance by directors, wordless and coming to terms with it. Instead, they want to *rewrite* their condition proactively.

Writers are most stupid when they believe they can purge themselves of their various traumas by writing through them. I suggest they read Freud on Da Vinci to find out sublimation is not so easy:

To become an artist, you might need a childhood fantasy of a vulture that "opened [your] mouth with his tail and struck [you] a few times with his tail against [your] lips," which you could only have if you were breastfed and somewhat closeted, etc. So what, painting is hard—the writer says—but artists *have* existed, there is no denying it.

— I've been working on this piece, the writer says.

— That relates to one of my own projects, the other writer responds, quickly forgetting to ask about the first writer's work.

— However, she continues, I'm not getting as much writing done as I would like.

— Ah, the second writer responds, back on track. It is important to make *habits*, you know, he says, as he always does, before describing his own routine, by way of which he has composed some 1,000 identically bad poems.

— You're right, the first writer admits with some guilt. She knows that it's important to create habits, but she also resents the advice, given that her mother is dying.

— Easier said than done, I suppose, he laughs, secretly suspicious that her mother's death might produce a "new" direction in her writing, and now jealous enough to inquire after the new work.

— What, he asks, with no intonation to suggest a question, is this new project.

A perverse side effect of the belief that writing will make you *feel better* is its corollary: the belief that, the more bad things happen to you, the more you'll have to write about.

The creative pursue real personal suffering in order to have the kinds of lives that merit autobiography, while the immoral take the opportunity to briefly imitate the suffering of others to access it in the first-person by proxy. Neither understands that the impossibility of pulling oneself out of poverty, say, is more integral to the experience than a week or two spent eating junk food because, someone just found out, it's cheaper per calorie.

Sophie, not yet fully acclimated to the life of the wealthy in the city to which she'd recently relocated, but happy to have moved away, once returned home for a summer. She looked for work.

She couldn't find work because 1.) The town had very little work that needs doing, 2.) What work there was wanted workers to linger for more than three months, 3.) What temp work there was could only be accessed by agencies who drug test, which she had forgotten, having moved to a city where her occasional pot habit couldn't hold a candle to the coke that lined classmates' keys.

But she persisted, finding one agency that leaves the drug test for the individual assignment. She offered evidence of her WPM and waited around, still stoned, hoping to perform some sort of data-entry.

She got a call: there was a one-day job at the ThyssenKrupp factory in quality control, from which she could make $132 in a twelve-hour shift. Relieved, Sophie borrowed her dad's car, drove to the factory, got a quick training: she'd be testing boxes of thousands of Phillips-head screws with the tip of a screwdriver to make sure it fit. She was told they'd found, on average, only five malfunctioning screws per 10K box, but that 1.) When a messed-up screw goes through the machine, it breaks a $600 part, and that both this risk and that 2.) Replacing the large quantity of screws they had already procured would cost a great deal more than paying $11/hour to test each screw by hand.

Luckily, Sophie was not alone: an older man who had been doing the job all week was seated across from her.

"I hope you're a talker," he introduced himself. "The last few haven't been, and it's a lot easier to get through this work if you can pass the time."

"I love to talk," she reassured him, grateful for his warnings. He was right that it would only take an hour for the wrists to start hurting, that smokers got more frequent breaks.

It doesn't take long for two people to establish the basic facts of their personal lives. They were both from this town; their families were, too; they were both struggling to find summer work; they both felt the same joy when a stranger was interested in going deep. Neither of them fit the narrative they were meant to expect of each other: he didn't understand why Sophie would be taking this job, if she were fancy enough to get into the Good School in the Distant City, and he called his friends over from the more permanent assembly lines to come meet this strange teenage girl.

He wanted something specific from her in return for this attention: advice. "How can I convince my daughter to go to college?" he asked. The other men with girls echoed this sentiment. His daughter was insisting on joining the military, having never liked school, and he didn't see the sense in signing up in the middle of a war everyone was coming to agree was Bad. The others wanted their daughters to leave their boyfriends, and college seemed like a good way for a girl to learn to whom she was superior.

The day carried on; Sophie smoked as many cigarettes as contractual breaks encouraged, trying to imagine what would convince another daughter that college life was preferable to death for one's country.

At 1AM, she left the industrial mall by the side street that connected it to the divided highway, onto which she turned the wrong way. The lights were out at the intersection, and her eyesight was hazy from staring at screws all day. She realized her mistake just as the oncoming traffic started veering around her, and, crying, she picked up her phone to call her dad to say goodbye. She tried to decide if a dad would prefer to hear his daughter die, or for her to die without hearing her again. Sophie didn't yet know about her panic attacks, believed herself just to be a dizzy person, so she was confused by her fading vision. The panic helped her ride through the stretch of road that lacked a grass meridian, though, which she noticed just in time to avoid a car that didn't have room to swerve.

The next day, she had dinner with another friend who had left town. This was the grounds of their new friendship: both having proven themselves snobs by moving away, they found in each other the ability to describe their prior year without risking implied judgment of their hometown.

Sophie told the friend the story of her half-day as a quality control tester, how what had stuck with her, after the panic left, after she had smoked all remaining cigarettes at the diner to calm down, was how she would never *have* to return. Her coworkers had been right that some set of occurrences had meant that one of the best jobs in town—still-unionized auto industry factory work—was one she was expected to find too painful, too tedious, to accept.

Her closeness to the friend ended when she responded: "You're so lucky, though! This will be an incredible experience to write about one day."

It's better for a writers to attempt to control their suffering by writing through it than to become tourists of pain.

So: creativity is hard. Freud wrote constantly, producing a nearly unreadable body of work (in terms of sheer quantity), and "the only beautiful thing" he ever wrote—by his own account, his interpretation of da Vinci by way of his diaries and his artwork—hinged on a misreading: the translator decided to rename the bird of Da Vinci's childhood fantasy, and Freud interprets the wrong bird. He finds a vulture in the garments of the painting of the Virgin, but to do so, he first finds it where it shouldn't have been: in the German translation of Da Vinci's diaries.

Say life takes your side and makes you an artist, a writer, a scientist, an inventor of a new style of thinking, a school: your greatest work will turn out to have relied on some small mistake.

If I could talk sense into my friends, I'd ask them to give up; I would tell them to enter the movies. With their lines written in advance, they would be freed from the anxiety of wordlessness—except where they were directed to express it—and freed too from the burden of getting over it.

Take Joey, one of my oldest friends, a writer whose fantasies of control are even bigger than most poet's: he's not only going to hash out his personal shit, his daily regrets. No, he wants to register world-historical shit, too—the young man seems to actually believe that by writing about the use of drones in contemporary warfare, the racist state of our prison system, or structural inequality more broadly, he'll support political resistance.

By getting him to admit that all of his problems centered around his frustrated relationship with masculinity—he wanted desperately to be manly as much as he sported a faux-radical misandry—it was easy to figure out which film best delivered the necessary proximity to violence alongside the hope of satisfying a woman to whom he had already proven himself inadequate.

It didn't take me long to identify exactly which film he should continuously relive, although it took much longer to convince him to stop writing. We deliberated one night over dinner and figured out it *had* to be Cary Grant's role in *His Girl Friday*.

I helped him hire a crew to recreate it, and he rewatches the movie at least once a week—sometimes the original and sometimes his own version, but always just before bed, to facilitate dreaming of the newspaper office.

As Walter Bruce, the young man gets to live out his true anxious fantasy—not of being a successful writer or sexual partner, but of being left by a wife for a much more boring man. In the original (as in the reenactment), Bruce's star reporter and ex-wife, Hildy Johnson, returns to the office from Reno to announce both her resignation and her new engagement, the latter set for the following day. Meanwhile, the newspaper needs someone to cover a developing story about a convicted murderer whose execution is as near-at-hand as Hildy's—or, at the very least, she's sentencing herself to life with an insurance salesman.

At once hero and cuckold, impossibly handsome and cast aside, my friend gets his wife back by showing her her *own* skills as a reporter, rather than by emphasizing his own. Along the way, he shows how undesirable her fiancé truly is, as the other man clearly wants her more stupid and bored.

One of the most difficult scenes for him to play out is the opening argument, where the exes establish both their continued desire and the ridiculous failure of their first attempt at love. Of course, he is forced to emulate Grant's coolheadedness—that's why this film is such a good treatment for his jealousy—but he suffers anew each time he hears her say she's remarrying because she "want[s] to go some place where [she] can be a woman." If he's failed to treat his wife like a woman, what does that make him?

At first, it seems only to make him into the employer he already was. He calls her "a newspaper man," and she says he treats her like "an errand-boy." At the same time, he's just a feminist: already, when she first expresses this desire to be a woman, he asserts: "I know what it would mean. It would kill you." Employers and feminists may be manly enough, but things go worse for him the second time around. About her new fiancé, she says, "He treats me like a woman," spelling it out. For Joey, this is taking things too far:

— He does, does he? How did I treat you—like a water buffalo?

— I don't know about water buffaloes, but I know about him. He's kind and sweet and considerate. He wants a home—and children.

— Say, sounds more like a guy I ought to marry. What's his name?

We have four relationships: 1.) Grant with his newspaperman: a simple employer/employee duo—that's fine. 2.) Grant with his ex-wife, whom he spared the marital role for her own sake, knowing she was cut out for something else—painful, but at least it casts him in a good light. 3.) Grant with a woman he failed to treat like one—this doesn't look as good. 4.) Grant with his ex-wife's fiancé—here, it seems that she has to be the newspaperman not just because she excels at it, but because he was busy preparing to be her wife.

This man's unwillingness to treat a partner as they ask is just right for Joey, but it's not the right role for everyone; that's why this method requires such careful decision-making when it comes to choosing the film.

My friend Alex, for example, an "aspiring novelist," needed just the opposite: to replay the role of a woman put in just the position she's requested.

— You can't get a guy going, then take refuge on the ice.

— Not my face! Not my hands!

— Murderer!

— Aren't you ashamed?

— I'm begging you to stop.

On my advice, Alex has been reliving this scene for the last two years. She suffers from recurring nightmares of rape, an inability to speak in public, a complex surrounding control that manifests in various physiological substitutes, an ambivalence with respect to her sexual identity, an inability to follow through on creative projects, and loose belly fat, among many other ailments, all of which have improved since she cast herself in the role of Erika in *The Piano Teacher*.

The choice of this film is obvious. First, and most importantly, it's about the horror of having to play out a scenario with only one possible narrative thread, especially in a script of one's own design: when her student rapes her in a scene that mirrors her original written fantasy, Haneke does not fuck around—there is no hand-wringing about her complicity or desire. Her desire is no longer at issue, which, as I have suggested, is the whole point of film therapy: staying with anxiety without the belief that you can do anything to get *through* it. Second, it's a film, which is to say, a fiction. By becoming Erika, she benefits from the constancy of this stress while ensuring the rape remains imaginary.

When this gets to be too much, I have her become the donkey in Robert Bresson's *Au hasard Balthazar*. She still gets a lot of beatings—and she still relearns that "love isn't everything"—but she reports finding the baptism scene really relaxing.

But why worry about writers?

Because, if they deserve the title, they're readers—and readers believe they can interpret their situations enough to make sense of them. If they aren't making sense, they blame themselves for a failure to have been sufficiently paranoid.

They need to learn that you don't read a book for the first time to interpret it. The purpose of the first reading is to make rereading possible, to render erotic the boredom of knowing what's coming.

And for another reason: because writers, as we'll see in the coming examples, love to seem poor.

The movies, everyone knows, are about money, even when they depict poverty. Then most of all, in fact, especially if you pay $15 to watch a multi-million dollar narrative about a poor protagonist, and especially if you yourself are poor, as poor people are less cheap and more willing to go to the movies. There are so many role models, in movies, of poor people who are forced to accept the fantasy of wealth their good-natured honesty is meant to reject.

Like Mary Smith in Mitchell Leisen's 1937 film *Easy Living*, which, as the name suggests, is a great movie about money, and about poverty. Mary's bound for the easy life. Here are some of the taglines that initially promoted it:

IT HAS NO RHYME . . . IT HAS NO REASON . . .
IT DOESN'T MAKE SENSE . . . IT MAKES LAUGHS!

It's dizzy—it's daffy—it's cockeyed—it's laughy!

This is already promising! Unlike the other film restagings, this one is sure to be enjoyable; by being senseless, it provides relief from the often-competing constraints of narrative coherence and pretension. As you can already tell, I must have a lot of love for the person who restages this role. Rather than getting assaulted or divorced, the right person for *Easy Living* gets to live in a screwball, get rich, fall in love, and learn to exist in a state of near-constant bewilderment.

Early in the film, Mary Smith (reassuringly generic—we already know this a role into which many could readily step) is fired from her shitty job at a magazine called *Boy's Constant Companion*—surprisingly, this is not porn—and turned out on the street with few prospects.

We're getting ahead of ourselves, though, as the movie first has to set up a reason for her dismissal. We open not with Mary, living difficultly, but with Mrs. Ball, living easily. And like many good movies, it ends the same place it begins (in this case, with a rich woman). As the opening credits roll, we watch Mrs. Ball slowly donning jewelry and flowers, and the shot fades to a close-up of a man's feet while his butler shines his shoes. There are workers everywhere: Mr. Ball stands before a door that opens onto a maid descending a ladder; a man sweeping the floor Mr. Ball walks onto; the butler dusting the back of his jacket while Mr. Ball keeps walking, as if too important to stop; the cleaning crew all moving out of the way to make way for his descent down the stairs, where, lacking their assistance, he stumbles head over heels towards his breakfast, which requires a table big enough for twelve, the companionship of an ungrateful son, more servants, and more hardboiled eggs than could possibly be eaten. Over breakfast, he reconciles his accounts, where he finds the purchase that sets the whole plot in motion: a bill for a $58K sable coat.

There's a confrontation. Mr. Ball addresses his wife as she sits before a mirror, and the camera captures her, her reflection, and his, but leaves the non-reflected husband out of frame—the overall visual impression is that he's been teamed up on by two of her. Men don't get women, or their coats. A series of closet doors, mirrored and cushioned, room dividers, etc., open and obstruct passage; the man trips over his own feet, slips headfirst under a vanity, knocked down by his own excesses—his quantity of stuff and staff impeding clear passage—as he chases his wife up mysterious stairwells, through the laundry another servant is hanging up to dry, to the edge of the roof, where he rips the extravagant fur from his wife's arms and tosses it over the side, right onto the head of our real protagonist, who is passing by on a streetcar below.

The feather of her hat is broken. She's angry, and it's a simple anger of inconvenience; she doesn't even consider the appeal of the coat responsible for the feather's breaking. Already, she fails to understand the fur's source; she even gets the direction from which it fell wrong, confronting the man behind her on the streetcar, whose own hat, a turban, remains unaffected by the fur's journey.

This is why this film is so helpful: as antidote to our desire to find meaning everywhere, and thereby control and even improve our way of living, we have the dramatic irony created by her inability to interpret anything that happens to her. Fur—always a reference at once to, at the very least, femininity, wealth, pubic hair, animals, cruelty, infidelity, glamour, sadism—is such an over-determined symbol that Mary's refusal to make anything of it at all reads as a joke.

Mary does not understand what the fur implies, but she does her best to return it. In the process, she meets Mr. J. B. Ball, the "Bull of Broad Street," who replaces her broken hat and insists she keep the coat he tossed off the roof.

She shows up to work in the sable. To her coworkers, the meaning of such an expensive fur is clear: she has a rich lover, and the office cannot keep on a girl of ill repute.

Much of the movie hinges on Mary's inability to read. She can neither identify the fur's worth—which she underestimates by some $57K—nor fully recognize that she has been misidentified as the mistress of a man, whom she also fails to recognize, to the extent that she manages to shack up with his son—whom she meets when he slums it at the automat—without noting the connection, shortly after moving into the posh hotel she's awarded for $7/night on the hotelier's hope that she'll put in a good word to her alleged lover.

In this, Mary resembles the cup and saucer in Oppenheim's surrealist *Le Déjeuner en fourrure*; the inoffensive femininity of the tea set is rendered obscene by furs.

So we have the movie, then. To get the girl who should live it, we just need to list what it offers its protagonist: the opportunity to know nothing, to have everything determined by actions other than her own, the folly of a poor person in

New York, the excessive polysemy of the signs she can't read, intrigue, unemployment, love.

Now, we have the reenacter too: already named Mary, in real life, already generically pretty. But from there, her current situation differs in all the ways that make this selection work. Rather than under-interpreting the signs that everyone else can read clearly, my friend's role as a soon-to-be-failed academic means that she's all-too-well-practiced in the art of finding meaning where it isn't. Rather than entering into the life of a kept woman by way of a *joie-de-vivre* that prevents the class-hatred that might get in the way of enjoying the beautiful hotel, she obtained just enough education to alienate herself from her past, and she's spent her life cultivating a disdain for luxury that makes her pissed when she gets near it. Limited to batty lines, open glances, and a way of rolling with the punches, by entering this film, Mary gets to live just how she needs to.

Sophie, on the other hand, posed a bigger challenge: certainly, she would be the friend most resistant to film therapy, not only because it required a degree of commitment— towards which she expressed not fear, but a genuine lack of acquaintance—but also because her relationship to *control*, to change, to anxiety, wasn't quite the same as the others. Which is to say, because she was somewhat less fucked, she was less interested in a method to which people generally turn out of lack of hope.

I could never get to her. Or I always could; Sophie always greets me with kindness, always hears me out, always asks questions in response to my rants that give me permission to keep going. But nothing touches her.

At the very least, I knew that she'd need to be in a more recent movie. In her own writing, she has specifically struggled to avoid the question of novelty or contemporaneity by imitating forms so already outdated that there was no risk of falling suddenly out of style, or accidentally employing an only-temporary fashion. She takes the same approach to clothes, avoiding this year's jeans by wearing only well-maintained classic dresses; she drinks and smokes like representations of past people, not like people themselves did; in short, because she has already cast herself in an old movie, she needs to recast herself in a new one.

When Sophie, too stoned, was watching S01E11 ("Out of Mind, Out of Sight") of *Buffy the Vampire Slayer*, she laughed at its opening with Shylock's speech—the English teacher, Ms. Miller, asking the class to relate a supposed earlier conversation about the "anger of the outcast in society" to "If you prick us, do we not bleed?"—this opening meant to foreshadow the episode's central problem, a girl who has gone invisible after being ignored for so long, who's now using her invisibility for murderous revenge.

She then remembered that, earlier in the night, she had tweeted: "Glad my cat daily reminds me: if you prick me, I do, in fact, bleed," thinking about a recent article she had read about the decline in stagings of Shakespeare in the prior century, which mentioned that popular culture still makes frequent reference to the soliloquies even if students mostly encounter the plays by way of allusion. She wrote a note on her whiteboard—"Read more Shakespeare?"—and then wrote below it, in a different color and smaller, "*find out how much Shakespeare most of your friends have read.*"

Initially, she laughed not at the coincidence, but at laughter itself: she had forgotten the "If you tickle us . . ." But her smile inverted as she remembered having watched (before giving in to the stoned depression of television) Lubitsch's 1942 *To Be or Not to Be*, where the most important recurring lines are not Jack Benny's (Hamlet's) but Felix Bressart's (Shylock's)—so that, in a Holocaust comedy, "Hath not a Jew eyes?" is played for laughs.

If a laugh is meant to prove one's quality, she now felt worthy, but also pursued.

When the *New York Times* reviewed *To Be or Not to Be* on its release, the critic, Bosley Crowther, could have stood to reread *Merchant of Venice*, since he couldn't recognize Lubitsch's juxtapositions in Shakespeare's: "It is hard to imagine how anyone can take, without batting an eye, a shattering air raid upon Warsaw right after a sequence of farce or the spectacle of Mr. Benny playing a comedy scene with a Gestapo corpse." The movie prioritizes the *do we not laugh* evidence over blood in laying claim to a life's merit.

Crowther ends his review of the film by complaining that its Jewish director is "a Nero, fiddling while Rome burns," recommending instead a documentary with "balance and feeling" by a "Stuart Legg"—a film, I imagine, with less blood and laughter, but where the documentarian shows how wonderful Britain has been in the fight against Germany. But Crowther can't quite admit he hates *To Be or Not to Be*, because the film includes the final screen appearance of its star Carole Lombard—a fact that requires "uncommon tact." For Lombard, blood won out over laughter: she died when the film was in post-production on a flight from a War Bonds Tour. Lubitsch struck one of her lines from the film after her death—"What can happen on a plane?"—out of respect, indicating a greater comfort with jokes about the ongoing mass murder than with jokes about one actress's early death. It's clear why, though. Lubitsch's characters imitate the Nazis on purpose, while Lombard predicts her own death by accident.

Coincidences are disrespectful. Lubitsch knew it, and so did Clark Gable, who had to ID the remains of his wife, mother, and friend because the former won the coin toss to determine whether they'd go home by train or plane. So did Sophie, who now had to read *Merchant of Venice* to determine whether she was being forewarned against something by encountering the line's repetition, or whether she merely lived in a language still too obsessed with the past for such repetitions not to happen a certain number of days each year.

For a girl of this nature, coincidences bore a heavy cognitive load. It took so many self-directed reminders not to find meaning in them, and she was much more comfortable with a life managed by some combination of "her own decisions" and "circumstance" that she couldn't take the fact that said life, occasionally, seemed to have a Writer, if one a bit heavy-handed with repeated allusions.

Sophie called me back. "I'm ready," she said. I needed little other explanation, even if resignation was a new note to hear in her tone.

I shook my head, disappointed that she was still angling for control, but I knew better than to disagree at such a rare moment. I let her tell me the whole above story, waiting for her to insist she belonged in *To Be or Not to Be* and waiting too for her characteristic indecision, which would surely lead her to slide from reference to reference. Of course, she'd first want to restage Anna Bronski's part, because getting to play an actress would seem to her a clever way out of agreeing to live out only one role. It wouldn't take long for her to see herself, instead, in *The Shop Around the Corner*, self-aware enough to know she would be just the kind of girl to scorn Jimmy Stewart IRL but fall desperately for him in correspondence, believing she was in control, but at every turn succumbing to plot; without noticing it, she'd then see herself instead as Meg Ryan in *You've Got Mail*, with a long explanation of how she'd rather do "ironic midnight movie" than "repertory" in her day-to-day life.

In the end, I didn't get the pleasure of a real consultation. We simply wound up at the movies with friends.

It was late afternoon, and we were getting high outside of the bank, in the brick square, fearful of confrontation by a cop or mother or asthmatic. Sophie was not nervous, though. She may have been right, but it's rude to be calm around someone who's panicking.

We went to see *Maps to the Stars*, which I had forgotten was by Cronenberg and had confused many times for the saccharine movie of a similar name playing concurrently, if in dissimilar theaters, about a young woman's mysterious ability to remain desirable in spite of her cancer.

To hide my anxiety from her, and to make sure I didn't accidentally make eye contact with anyone who might otherwise have overlooked me, I pulled my hat down farther. It was a new hat, I should say, and I am almost as evangelical about acquiring hats as I am about reliving movies; of course, hats mostly live in film, now, so there's no real disagreement. Sophie should have acquired a simple linen summer cap, the sort of hat that could be procured effectively in any price range, but which is implausible to wear off the beach.

She was wearing no hat at all.

People's current attitude towards hats betrays a larger cultural problem: our despicable faith in self-knowledge. "I'm not a hat person," they say, with a sense of banal confidence normally reserved for observations about currently occurring weather events. They don't even bother to modify their self description with "so far" or "yet" or "because" or even "having made a thorough effort" or "and I don't give enough fucks to try."

Being stoned and wearing a hat at the movies can be stressful. But it can also be pleasant, especially if you sit in the back row and have no need to worry about obstructing anyone's view. It would be difficult to describe this movie as pleasant, though, given the sheer amount of cruelty and creepy family interactions—even if, at the same time, we all have a sense of cruelty's pleasantness.

I knew what she'd say.

— *Ugh*, Elsie—*No one* in that film was likeable.

As if likability were the most important thing, in movies, love, or hats.

— It was creepy and even sort of good, she would go on, but I don't really want to watch rich Hollywood types work out their Oedipal complexes while living fabulously.

I let her go on. It's important to do so, sometimes.

— I can't even get a shit therapist, she complained, to take my insurance, so she can tell me to keep track of my anxiety on a scale of 1–10.
— Sophie.
— Yes?
— This is the perfect movie for you.
— Ha, fuck you! You like me that little? Do tell me which of those shits I'm supposed to be.
— No.

I explained: it was exactly her need to be liked, her fear of becoming unsympathetic, that made this selection right. Even better, the film was about fame, which the young poet obviously wanted, but had chosen a form that could never produce it.

But which character? Her question was the right one, as Sophie's so often are.

Sophie wakes up. She prepares, again, as she must every day, to become Dr. Stafford Weiss (John Cusack), the therapist of Havana (Julianne Moore), the man who leads her through reenactments of childhood memories and weird pilates. By *being* the absurd therapist, she lives out the anxiety of finding her own therapist in real life, one who might threaten to take her symptoms away, and her personality with it. And who would try to replace them with strategies for productivity, at work or in her relationships. She makes others relive their childhoods instead of living her own; she abandons her own daughter in the process—in fact, she pretends never to have experienced the daughter at all.

Sophie wakes up. She begins preparing, as she always does, for her role as Benjie.

Sophie wakes up. She is the real main character, according to many reviews: the poem that repeats throughout the film, Paul Eluard's "Liberté." That is, she is not the poem, but she is Eluard's writing as limited to the lines of that poem that appear in the mouths of the characters she's already considered being.

Sophie wakes up. She's the movie's closed captioner, rendering all the characters' styles concise.

Etc.

Etc.

Sophie also soon found herself reliving the lives of the actors themselves—at first by playing out their parts, of course, but eventually by slipping into their personal lives, into other works, into the lives of their fans, etc.

Of course, she couldn't do this literally—you can't hire a film crew to make you, for example, live as an orphan across various Flatbush apartments, with some combination of sisterly encouragement and personal drive ultimately leading you to change your name to Barbara Stanwyck—but she could read biography after biography, taking walks that would retrace character's paths.

She got out at the Newkirk station on the Q train, where some orange toms crossed her path. She frowned, wondering if cats roamed early-twentieth-century Flatbush, remembered her longstanding plan to take in an orphaned street cat and name it Desire, chose one particular cat to follow, and did so for a few blocks before remembering she was meant to be following Stanwyck, *née* Ruby Stevens. She took a long walk over to Rogers, where it looked less like she imagined Flatbush looked a hundred years earlier than it did among the old Victorians, but she thought this was more "accurate" anyway; the Flatbush where Stevens/Stanwyck grew up had changed dramatically in the prior century, and she couldn't imagine the young starlet walking any streets that had stayed the same for generations.

At first, I was furious with Sophie. Her outright rejection of the very process she had set out to try was so like her, but so frustratingly apt, that I could only read it as an act of hostility.

Of course *I* would be limited to a duller version of my own idea—living through anxiety without attempting to get rid of it—while she would quickly see a more complicated way, something maintaining the relationship to scripts and to repetition without needing to do so literally (and so expensively—film equipment is not cheap). Ever insistent that any good strategy ought to be available to all classes, she quickly moved from character to character until she returned to the subtitling role, her preferred job among the ones she'd tried.

Sophie threw *Jeanne Dielman* at me, insisting that women have tried "film therapy" for as long as they've "kept house," steadily repeating the roles that cause their anxiety in the hope that they grow accustomed to hell. They wake up and find their son's shoes while he's still sleeping, get them ready for him to enter the world, spend all day planning a meal they don't look forward to and don't care for, fuck if they have to, if that's how they maintain their lives, and, hopefully, commit murder.

Soon Sophie had developed still further strategies beyond mine, and had begun to write to me about them; above all, she needed to prove that the act of writing was not incompatible with the act of accepting one's lack of control. She came up with a series of procedures to carry out, but there was one she could never bring herself to do, in a way that surprised both of us.

"You say we shouldn't bother to write in the absence of any real control," she said. "I say, fuck that." So she wrote me a story.

"Silent Treatment," by Sophie

Sophie's not-talking this week was somehow more un-nerving than the always-talking that constitutes so much of the other fifty-one. She made coffee in silence; she drank it in silence; she ordered it in silence—by apologetically slipping a note across the counter that read "1 small coffee, no room"—and she sat, in silence, across from you, looking as if she expected you to talk anyway.

This was all extremely annoying, anyone would agree, he thought. Silent, she seemed even stupider, younger; she dressed more colorfully, with more care for the materials than for her appearance; she didn't cook him dinner, or lunch, or make the bed after she woke up. Before and after this silent treatment, as he called it, she woke up after him, still sleepy, which he used to find beautiful, but which now, especially *now*, looked selfish, like a childish refusal to do what others do, a stupid posture that relied on groggy morning whispers to overcome itself.

He tried to return the quiet favor, but felt himself, despite his earlier protests, coming to understand that the way he was normally silent only towards her (as opposed to her undiscrim-inating dumbness) was, in fact, an act of hostility.

Though he resented the change, it wasn't as if he had something to say to her. He was mostly angry, in fact, about this revelation, that he had only ever spoken in response to her speaking. He found in her "peaceful" "introspective" sitting-still the anxiety she must experience in everyday life with him. In short, she had failed to make up for his emptiness, and she had thereby forced him to miss her.

Silence journal:

Somewhat sad. Hungrier than usual. Cheeks slightly discolored, as if underslept.

I thought the hardest part would be failing at social situations, but it's not so bad—

at the very least (I think this is right?) I don't have to worry whether I have said the right thing.

I find myself reading a lot more often—that part is the best—and thinking about a thing I can't write down yet.

Yet, he was still better than her.

He would not keep complicated spreadsheets and drawings of the way his body responded to silence, smiling while he noted that, when asked a question he could not respond to with words, he did not compensate with gestures but instead stood still, as if the body's movement only followed speech.

She, meanwhile, had already broken her promise to herself by writing imaginary conversations she wished she could have with him:

— I don't want life to be so clean—"I love you, good morning"—½ can twice a day, one of us remembering to close the curtains when the sun is hot.

— Me either, Sophie.

— Do you really mean it?

— At night, I don't want to drink the right amount to only kiss whom I'm supposed to kiss—I don't mind this during the day, though—

— The train comes just as we get on the platform, every day.

— Exactly. Or when it doesn't, we have our books ready, or we hold hands.

— And I never forget to come home to you.

— I want to forget.

— But I don't want to ruin our life.

— You won't. Instead, you will kiss women.

— And you will live in neither cities nor towns. You will find out how to have left the town you grew up in without having gotten anywhere.

— I will wake up in the arms of someone else's dog.

— The drain is still clogged.
— Meow. Meow. Meow. Meow. Meow. Meow. Meow.
— Miss. *Hello*, miss. You are beautiful.
— Excuse me.
— Do you support gay rights?
— Nice tits.
— Hey gorgeous.
— Room for milk?
— That's $3.75. 10, 15, 16.25. Have a good rest of your day.
— Excuse me.
— After you.

— There's a phone call for you, Sophie.

... What do you want me to do? Take a note?

... Sophie's not available right now.

... He says it's urgent, Sophie.

... Well, you can talk *at* her, but she won't respond. Don't ask me.

—Hello? Sophie?

... This is ridiculous.

... Fine, I am just calling to tell you that the plumber can only make it today at 4.

... Can you come home from work early?

... OK, please be here—I can't. I'll try to give him as many details as possible in a note. If you cannot make it, fuck, I don't know, call me back after I hang up and I'll interpret the silence.

... This is really fucking selfish of you, you know? I'll see you at home.

— Please get the report to me before you leave at 6 today.

… Excuse me? 4? OK, get it to me by 4 then. Are you going to stay late tomorrow to make up the hours? Alright.

— That is a beautiful hat.
— Sexy. Sexy girl.
— Excuse me.

"I'm Stacy—I'm here about the clog."

The plumber was beautiful, Sophie thought; she made the hallway open out behind her.

Stacy had come braced for an angry man's shit, since her boss had warned her that the guy who made the appointment sounded like an asshole. Instead, here was a girl answering the door in a small dress, like so many had before.

Sophie did not respond, but stared blankly at her in a way that conveyed just little enough to leave room for the best interpretations: her nails were short enough; she only broke eye contact to check out Stacy's uniform. At the same time, it looked like a one bedroom apartment.

Stacy followed Sophie's clumsy gesture towards the bathroom and got to work inserting the snake into the clump of hair, mold, and soap residue that made up the only willing comingling of this couple's mornings. When she was done, she looked for the girl in the kitchen to leave her the bill, but instead found a note addressed to her with a blank, signed check beside it.

The top of the note, now scratched out, was written in very clear, all-caps print, and had described the nature of the clog as if anticipating a reader who wouldn't understand. She did not like its writer from its writing. In its place, or rather, just below its place, in the same pen but a different hand, now read:

Dear Stacy,

First, please let me apologize for my rudeness. As a project of personal improvement (that does not, so far, appear promising), I have decided to take a week off of speaking.

In general I have forbidden myself even notes like these explaining the silence, but I am making an exception because:

1. I am considering this an "edit" of the already existing note explaining the problem, and editing is not the same as producing text, and because

2. I feel the need the address you, and most examples of ritualistic abstinence allow exceptions in cases of need.

   I do feel that I need you. I am sure of this, more than I am sure that it is helpful to be quiet for a week at a time, or to go for enough walks, or to make sure that I take the time to breathe slowly and eat slowly and pay attention to my other needs.

3. Specifically, I need you to go back into the bathroom, open the bottom drawer in the plastic shelving unit, and find the large black box in the back behind the spare towels. Inside the box is a strap-on that would be *perfect* for you. I saw you and I thought, 'I want her cock inside me, and I feel as though I've already had it.' I do not care whether you put this on over or under your clothes, but do put it on.

   Perhaps you are not comfortable wearing a strap-on. I could be wrong. But somehow, I'm confident.

4. Once you are ready, open the door on your right, put your hand over my mouth, and fuck me. You can do whatever else you want—and you can, of course, tell *me* to do whatever you/I want—but it would be great if you could keep my mouth covered. You could take off your underwear and gag me with it, for example. I want you to make me scream, but I don't want to be able to produce sounds.

5. If you do this for me, it can end however you like—we could go have a weird lunch in silence, or you could simply put the strap-on back underneath the towels and go.

6. I understand, of course, if you are straight, horrified, or otherwise not interested. In that case, please write out a check to yourself in the amount I owe you for the clog, so that I don't have to face your rejection.

7. But if you do agree to this, know that I am really looking forward to filling out that check.

Sincerely,
Sophie

Stacy was, indeed, interested.

(The bank teller later rejected the check on account of its smeared, illegible numbers, and she had to stop by later that week for a new check. The man who answered the door apologized for his girlfriend's clumsiness, and she gulped.)

Sophie's not-talking this week was very interesting.

Sophie was always up to something, they agreed.

The party last week was great.

Work was fine, but they weren't sure they were really pursuing their *careers*, you know; so-and-so had just gotten hired at X business; Y had moved to Smaller City on account of stress.

Yeah, yeah, their cats were adjusting well to the heat.

They wondered how her boyfriend was handling her silence, and their eyes got big.

They both looked beautiful today.

They talked, over drinks, about how *they* would handle *their* involvement in Sophie's new "project": when they had dinner with her tomorrow, would they try to forget that she was being silent and address her the way they always did? Would they take the opportunity to say whatever it was to her they might have found themselves not otherwise saying? Would there be a recording device, and if so, how would their voices sound? Should they smoke excessively this evening to give tomorrow's voices a more impressive timbre? Yes, they definitely should.

They gossiped. He had not kissed her yet, and they had already had three dates. Did they even count as dates at this point? Did Sophie and George have a decent sex life, they wondered? What was it like to fuck a silent person? They moved their drinks to the tables outside, chain-smoked, and made small talk while imagining the shape of each others' breasts.

They imagined, too, the shape of the other women's breasts on the street, and as the red rose higher in each of their cheeks, they suspected each other of an attraction to Sophie that threatened to overshadow their attraction to each other, of which they also suspected each of their own selves.

Because her friends had been warned. To anyone not Sophie, it was clear that this altered the experiment too fundamentally; if part of the goal was transcribing a record of others addressing her, she must have been looking forward to, or at least planning on, the angry, confused interactions with people who could not make sense of a normally friendly girl's sudden refusal to communicate. But she wanted the silence for herself, not for them, and she hated to be rude. For this reason, she carried business cards explaining the situation, which she would pass out as a last resort.

The cat meowed. Her written record of everything addressed to her was made up largely of transcribed meows, chirrups, purrs, growls, hisses, lurps, and yowps. Certainly, the cat spoke more than the boyfriend. In a week that was meant to reveal a new kind of listening by turning herself into an input-only audio device, Sophie probably found herself newly processing only the unlistened-to parts of her cat's monologue. Most people, that is, were sensitive enough to respond to her silence in kind. Although this was changing for *him*, as her new-found silence provided him a surprising opportunity to lecture. This is what you are always fucking like—he would say—

— You decide something is a good idea, and whether or not it drives me crazy, you'd rather do the stupid thing than actually make yourself useful.

… What do the people at work think?

… If you lose your job for this shit, I am not supporting you.

… I hope you do lose your job.

… The walk home will be especially lonely, since you won't be able to call anyone.

… What if a man on the street attacks you? There'd be onlookers, ready to intervene, but your silence would read like acquiescence—you're so fucking stubborn, I bet you'd stick to your silence while he raped you, slowly, even tenderly, against the door of our own apartment building. It'd look to everyone else like two lovers carried away. They'd probably all masturbate thinking about it later, even, not yet doubting what they saw. Later, sure, it'd enter into their heads to wonder whether they witnessed a rape, but just as their leg muscles relaxed.

… I hate you.

The cat did not even need to vocalize: it could head-butt her, pee, rub its cheeks against the furniture, or bite the hand that feeds. Sophie's ears drew back, and the small blonde hairs down her spine stood up, as she slightly wiggled her tailbone. But he did not see it.

— Just one this evening?

… Excuse me, miss. Three? You're meeting people, OK, go right on it.

— Can I get you anything to drink?

— Sophie! Oh my god. How are you? How is your project? Shit! [laughing]

… I guess we can't ask questions, Hannah.

— You look super pretty, Sophie. Silence becomes you! No, really.

— This is already unnerving. I need a drink.

— Emily. Let's get right down to it.

She did not need to *learn* to be stubbornly, childishly silent—quiet only on a whim. She needed, rather, to learn how to interrupt herself with silence, how to be comfortable with the necessarily occasional aspect of her own role in conversation. This project was nothing but a futile hope for some kind of reward, he tried to explain, a replacement for other givings-up she was avoiding: her lover, her job, her country, even smoking, to be honest—"You haven't gone a week without smoking since our first session, yet you can be silent for seven days: doesn't that seem significant to you?" In his professional opinion, he had advised strongly against the plan, and saw it as the most obvious sort of acting out.

As a therapist, he knew this must be his fault. They had their session tomorrow, at which nothing would be said at all by either. He had to prepare himself for that.

— Good morning, Sophie.

… See you next week, Sophie.

George was wrong about the people at work. They

— You missed a call, Sophie

either respected the clear separation between the office and life that seemed exaggerated by this kind of decision,

— Watch out

or, they had that separation so effectively themselves that they never thought about

> — [With an understanding smile] Can we set up a meeting for when you 'get your voice back' on Monday?

her or they were secretly

> — So I can say anything to you and won't stop me?

in love with her.

But it wasn't just that they were nice—they also valued her too much to question her judgment.

She had recently made a major suggestion at the office that had earned her a lot of her colleagues' respect: it had been only on a whim that she proposed they get involved in the pilot program for this new government service, wherein small businesses or individuals could submit free information requests for lost digital information or phone conversations stored in the archives of the NSA.

It was an elegant solution: the government was turning the tides on opposition to the mass collection of private data, and they had done so by making that collection a useful service: *Spill coffee on your laptop?* The NSA would restore your data. *Accidentally wipe your cellphone of contacts?* The NSA would auto-update for you. *Curious whether your husband was stepping out?* They'd cross-reference his correspondence for you. The government was advertising it as an automatic, global backup hard drive, but it was already being used by suspicious lovers and terrorists alike.

— If I can *say* anything without you stopping me, what will you stop me from *doing*?

When the office's networked shared storage failed, along with its backup, in the middle of a large project that week, it was Sophie who spoke to a polite, Midwestern-sounding government agent, and who saw the files restored by the end of the day.

After this success, she brainstormed ways to make use of this service for her silence project; she was sure microphones had picked up the majority of the words, for example, that had been addressed to her that week. So far, she had failed to transcribe all of the words coming her way; she thought being quiet would make it easier, but she was too caught up identifying the patterns of quiet and frustration and desire to remember to record.

Although most calls went recorded but obviously unheard, a college-era arrest at a protest had resulted in Sophie's being given a Personal Listener, one of hundreds of thousands of government employees assigned to specific security risks. He had already sent out a security alert about her silent responses to phone calls, which she continued to pick up all week long.

The man assigned to listen to Sophie's calls knew even better than Sophie, her friends, and her therapist that her boyfriend was wrong about a lot. George believed her boring, vaguely stupid, faithful to a fault, and scatter-brained, whereas her NSA file proved her to be a cheating bitch, though one well-loved by both personal and professional connections.

The agent had a lot on his plate right now. He spent his workday hoping to find evidence that Sophie was leaving George, even though he was assigned to find evidence of something else.

It did not help that he had not been told what else, and only encouraged to keep his suspicions completely open to all possibilities; he believed that she was suspected of the highest levels of government betrayal. That is, he assumed that a woman who strayed from love would stray from her country, especially when both were such obvious pieces of shit; he assumed she had knowledge and influence well beyond his own, which were equivalent only to a security clearance and not to a relationship; he suspected, from what he could make out on his recordings, that she was capable of communicating with animals, and was nervous about how to report this to higher-ups without risking his job.

To be fair, it appeared to the agent that George was so unaware of Sophie's successes because, even when she was in her normal state of over-communication, she never mentioned them.

As he fell further in love with Sophie, the agent thought increasingly about why she refused to let her boyfriend know about anything good that happened to her. He assumed it was because of her disappointment at being excluded from the pilot dream-transcription program, which, unlike the backup hard drive program, kept its participants completely in the dark about their involvement. To prevent people discovering they were involved, the CIA had an annual open application period, and sent a few select acceptance notifications only to people who were not actual participants; the rest, including the dreamers themselves, received kind rejections.

The NSA's data-collection program's main function was to increase public support for intelligence collection. At this, it was effective—people were grateful enough for the convenience of universal shared storage to give up the generally preferable ignorance of being watched. The government was making the same tradeoff, anyway; in exchange for the program's popularity, officials accepted that it increased public awareness of surveillance, and could feasibly result in people taking greater care with encryption. While some conservatives used this to argue against the program's being discussed in public forums, everyone knew that the encryption wars could no longer be won by trying to hide the fact of surveillance itself.

Not so for the dream program, even if its more creative element might have presented an opportunity to get artists and writers on board. Secrecy was key. The feds already assumed that people were communicating differently, knowing they were being overheard. While they accepted this for a program whose real purpose was public buy-in, they couldn't permit a similar side effect for the dream program, which already relied on such messy data. Their team of psychoanalysts had warned them about the way recording dreams produced new dreams in response, so participants' awareness (or access to their own records), it only followed, could harm the validity of future dreams' interpretation.

But there was a still-bigger concern. As the first transcriptions came in, they verified a prior hypothesis: that classified information was being accidentally revealed to dreamers in the night.

Sophie's not-talking was lovely for the inhabitants of her dreams, who, living only for the hours of the night she set aside for them, found themselves always changing by way of the changes produced in her: when she started new diets, vices, affairs, or habits, they changed and grew in number; they moved with the regularity of her bowels and heartbeat, with the number of animals she touched each day—and above all, of course, sleep. If those whose existence was more, as far as they could hazard, independent of hers, found the silence inconvenient, they were enjoying a moment of radical self-discovery.

It had been a few years since she had begun joining them each night, bringing with her all the accessories of her dream world, which called itself "Bernadette Elijah Rafael," or *the place of saying*. When she first showed up, they also showed up, it had seemed, although with memories of lives they had no impression of having lived out yet, constituted by a certain constellation particular to each: an important blanket under which they had each slept better than any other (all them the kind of weave that leaves a negative pattern on the underside, all of them sleeping better still when that side faced out and the "true" image wrapped around their legs in the night); a creature that had seemed, in childhood, to have preferred them to others; a fight with their mothers; a small subset of sexual acts whose physical realization could be somewhat recalled; no photographs—they had each, separately, apparently lived without photographs, even though they had favorite movies, all of them on religious themes; one sibling each; and a view from a window. There was little else. They had only what Sophie needed them to have, and yet they acquired new things, gradually became more individual, even during the sixteen hours each day they seemed to not exist.

She was with them more now. She was even more beautiful than they had imagined she could be. She left her silence behind when she joined them, and brought in its place something it must have generated: she gave them presents of new creatures, more trees, additional walls to the rooms they lived in—a more populated world. And while many of them cradled the beautiful, squash-faced kitten

—«Hello Sophie's dream friends, I prefer to be scratched *here*, thank you so very much! and by the way, there is a secret to history the human world is too stupid to recognize»—

the others sat at the long, irregularly shaped table, and took turns standing on it, finally disappearing with Sophie to another, more temporary place.

"Sophie Torre? I'm here to speak with you about a possible opportunity."

Sophie smiled apologetically, but was already in the process of closing the door when he wedged his foot in it.

"Are you not Sophie? There's no need to be afraid, Miss."

Her smile remained, but its remaining also gave it a different meaning. She did not speak.

"You've already guessed that I'm with the government, but surely that doesn't give you reason to be afraid. You're a patriot, no?"

In Sophie's dream world, George had somehow infiltrated, and he was sitting on Sophie's back, looking from that higher position down onto the creatures that were meant to be only hers, unconsciously holding her mane in his hand too tightly, too careless to think to help swat the flies off of her skin.

"Leave this place, man," they insisted.

"But I only just got here," grimacing in what he must have thought was a smile, "do you faeries not have any sense of fucking hospitality?"

The floor of the room was made entirely of wood, in planks—she had never seen this before—she was hungry—she bucked up onto her hind legs and danced a little, as she loved to do—she did not even feel his weight leave her back, she was so strong—but she did hear his bones snap, and she laughed.

"It is OK to be a horse," she said to her friends.

"That is true. A horse is a good thing to be."

"But, Sophie"—and the words were all she could handle; as they moved closer to dialogue, the image went away and was replaced only by the texture of voices. Then she saw the lights of his eyes go out, and she would have swished her tail, if she still had a body—"Isn't there something we're supposed to be doing here?"

"OK. I see that someone has tipped you off. Is there somewhere we can speak privately?"

And Sophie led him into the bedroom, gestured to the places she suspected cameras to be hidden, and shrugged.

"I don't know how you heard about this project in advance of this conversation—and to come on board you will eventually have to disclose that—but you already seem to have begun the task I've been sent to commission you for. Excuse me a moment, Miss."

When he returned looking all the more concerned, Sophie did her best to convey her confusion without speaking. She eventually got across to the agent the relevant information: that yes, she was already in the middle of an experimental durational silence that she had no intention of breaking early; that yes, it had already had a dramatic effect on the content of her dreams; but that no, she was not aware that either of these facts supported the ongoing government research for which she was to be commissioned.

She learned that her dreams had, in fact, been monitored for the last ten years, much longer than the technology for dream surveillance was supposed to have existed. Specific dreams she'd had in the previous few days had triggered an alarm, and they wanted to use her as a subject to record information apparently being revealed at night to those unusually quiet during the day.

He saw her looking at the clock anxiously, and asked her how long until her initial week was up. She held up three fingers of her right hand and formed a zero with the fist of her left. They sat in silence for the half hour, waiting for her to be able to ask the questions she inevitably had.

Sophie spoke first:

— Why is the moon on fire?

— Excuse me?

— How long has the moon been on fire?

Sophie wasn't worried about the moon, though: she was in a rush to get back to work on her writing.

She refused to participate in the program, shrugging as he threatened her with legal reprisals. With sadness, she found a drug to take away her dreams, said goodbye to the animals in *Bernadette Elijah Rafael*, told them to take care, quit her job, left her boyfriend, called Stacy, moved in, went for a walk, watched movies, waited.

Diana Hamilton is the author of *The Awful Truth*, *Okay, Okay, God Was Right*, and *Shit Advice Columnist*, as well as some chapbooks. She writes poetry, fiction, and criticism about style, crying, shit, kisses, dreams, fainting, writing, and re-reading. You can walk through audio recordings of her dreams in the first-person shooter by Alejandro Miguel Justino Crawford, *Diana Hamilton's Dreams* (Gauss PDF), a sister project to *The Awful Truth*.

She published her earliest books with The Dolphin Publishing Co. at Davis Park School in Terre Haute, Indiana, where her subjects included cops' suicides, abusive relationships, escaped polar bears, and grief. In 1996, her bio indicated that she hoped to grow up to be a teacher and writer and live in Duluth, Minnesota. Instead, she now teaches writing in New York, where she lives with the poet Shiv Kotecha and the cat, Émile, a.k.a. Monster. She received her PhD in Comparative Literature from Cornell University, where she tried to determine what "style" is.

Golias Books seeks to promote and circulate poetry that avails itself of a diverse array of registers, modes, genres, and formal possibilities—poetry that traffics in the remoter realms of what has traditionally been called poetics. We are interested in longer poems that develop more extended narrative or discursive arcs than that of the dilatory epiphany, in poetry as argument or architecture or assemblage, in poetry that *means* and *does* rather than poetry that *expresses*. At the same time, while the lessons of the previous few generations' emphasis on experimentation are well taken, we seek to explore an intuition that something of value may have been lost along with earlier humanisms' concern with ethical, political, and aesthetic judgment; therefore, while abjuring reactionary or conservative atavisms, we are interested in revitalizing historical poetic forms that may help us expand the narrow demesne within which contemporary poetry largely confines itself.